THE Girls WHO Dish™!

Seconds Anyone?

THE Girls WHO Dish™!

Seconds Anyone?

Whitecap Books

Vancouver / Toronto / New York

Whitecap Books
Vancouver/Toronto

Edited by Elaine Jones
Proofread by Elizabeth McLean
Front cover photograph by Lionel Trudel
Back cover photograph taken by Greg Athans at Aqua Riva Restaurant
Interior photographs by Greg Athans
Cover design by Tanya Lloyd
Interior design by Warren Clark

Printed and bound in Canada

Canadian Cataloguing in Publication Data

The girls who dish

Includes index.
ISBN 1-55110-945-X

1. Cookery. I. Barnaby, Karen.
TX715.6.G5932 1999   641.5   C99-910843-3

The publisher acknowledges the support of the Canada Council and the Cultural Services Branch of the Government of British Columbia in making this publication possible. We acknowledge the financial support of the Government of Canada through the Book Publishing Industry Development Program for our publishing activities.

Contents

Soups

Salads

Vegetables

Entrées

Desserts

Pet Snacks

Foreword

Bravo! The "girls who dish" received rave reviews for their cookbook premiere. Food critics were delighted, home cooks received standing ovations for their dinner parties, and guests rushed out to buy the hot new cookbook by these dynamite women chefs from Vancouver. From the moment they launched their book, everyone sensed their high level of energy and vitality, as they dished up impressive signature recipes that sent our taste buds soaring. Within weeks of hitting the bookstores, *The Girls Who Dish* became a Canadian bestseller.

It is now time for an encore. *The Girls Who Dish: Seconds Anyone?* delivers more fine recipes—each bearing the distinctive stamp of the chef who created it. Who could resist dishes such as Chèvre and Pear Quesadillas with Cilantro Crema, Smoke and Lime Chicken Soup, Grilled Asparagus with Grapefruit Vinaigrette, Après-Ski Skillet of Potatoes, Peppers and Feta, Curry-Crusted Leg of Lamb with Cumin Raita, and Banana Chocolate Chiffon Cake with Bourbon Cream?

I know I'm looking forward to mixing and matching recipes from both books for my friends and family. The "girls who dish" make it simple for us—generously sharing their culinary secrets so we can all cook like the pros!

—Diane Clement

Appetizers

Roasted Garlic and Chive Crackers

This recipe makes 6 large round crackers designed for sharing at the table or piling high on a buffet table. To get the crackers crisp, I use a flat ceramic tile, called a pizza stone. Try serving these crackers with Chèvre Torte, Tapenade *or* Smoked Black Cod Brandade *from our* first Girls Who Dish *cookbook.*

Makes 6 crackers		Mary Mackay
3/4 cup	lukewarm water	180 mL
1 1/2 tsp.	honey	7.5 mL
2 Tbsp.	chopped chives	30 mL
5	cloves roasted garlic, mashed	5
1 3/4 cups	white bread flour	420 mL
1/4 tsp.	dry instant yeast	1.2 mL
1/2 tsp.	fine sea salt	2.5 mL
	coarse sea salt to taste	

In the bowl of a heavy-duty mixer, combine the water, honey, chives and roasted garlic. In a separate bowl, measure heaping spoonfuls of flour into measuring cups and level off for a total of 1 3/4 cups (420 mL). Do not scoop the flour directly out of the bag or you will get a different amount. Stir in the instant yeast and fine sea salt. Add the flour mix to the bowl of the mixer. Using a dough hook, mix on low speed for 3 minutes. Increase the speed to medium and mix another 4 minutes. The dough should be moist and sticky.

Place the dough in a large greased bowl and cover with plastic wrap. Let rise in a warm draft-free place until doubled in bulk, about 3 hours.

Divide the dough into 6 equal portions. Cover with plastic wrap and let rest for 15 minutes. Roll each piece into a 1/8-inch-thick (.3-cm) circle. Place on non-stick baking paper.

Preheat a pizza stone or a baking sheet on the lowest shelf of a 500°F (260°C) oven.

Mist the top of the crackers with water and sprinkle with coarse sea salt. Place 2 crackers on the pizza stone. Bake until crisp, about 5–8 minutes. Crackers can be stored in a plastic container, tightly covered, for a few days.

Porcini Mushroom Mascarpone Crostini

In North America crostini have reached new heights and come topped with everything from scallops to tapenade. These mushroom crostini are great—they can be used not only as an hors d'oeuvre but paired with salad greens they make a delicious first course or luncheon dish.

Makes 2 dozen		Lesley Stowe
1/4 cup	dried porcini mushrooms	60 mL
4 Tbsp.	unsalted butter	60 mL
1 tsp.	minced garlic	5 mL
1 Tbsp.	minced shallot	15 mL
3 cups	trimmed and sliced button mushrooms	720 mL
1/2 tsp.	minced fresh thyme	2.5 mL
2 Tbsp.	brandy	30 mL
1/3 cup	heavy cream	80 mL
1/4 cup	mascarpone cheese	60 mL
1/2 tsp.	sea salt	2.5 mL
1/4 tsp.	freshly cracked black pepper	1.2 mL
24	1/4-inch-thick (.6-cm) slices baguette	24

Soak the dried mushrooms in warm water for at least 20 minutes. When they are soft, drain. Check the stems for sandy deposits; cut off and discard. Slice the mushrooms into 1/2-inch (2.5-cm) pieces.

Melt the butter in a sauté pan. Add the garlic and shallot, and gently sauté until the garlic is soft, about 5 minutes. Add the porcini and button mushrooms and the thyme. Increase the heat and sauté until the mushrooms are cooked through, about 10 minutes. Add the brandy and allow it to evaporate. Add the cream and cheese, bring to a boil, lower the heat and simmer for 2 minutes to thicken and reduce the cream. Add the salt and pepper, and reduce the heat to keep the mixture warm.

Toast both sides of the bread under the broiler. Divide the mushroom mixture equally among the slices and serve immediately.

Grilled Mushroom, Eggplant and Olive Flatbread

I love the balance of flavours and textures in this flatbread. The sweet eggplant carries the salty olives and the slightly charred mushrooms. This can be served as a main course with Mediterranean Salad with Tapenade Vinaigrette (page 53) or a simple green salad.

Serves 4 to 6		Karen Barnaby
3 Tbsp.	extra virgin olive oil	45 mL
2 lbs.	eggplant, peeled and cut into 3/4-inch (2-cm) slices	900 g
3/4 lb.	oyster mushrooms, thick stems removed	340 g
1/8 tsp.	salt	.5 mL
1/2 lb.	green Colossal olives, pitted and coarsely chopped	227 g
3	cloves garlic, minced	3
1–2	dried hot chili peppers, finely chopped	1–2
1 tsp.	fresh thyme leaves	5 mL
	salt and freshly ground black pepper to taste	
	cornmeal, for sprinkling on the baking sheet	
1 recipe	Mary Mackay's Pizzas Vertes dough (page 132)	1 recipe

Preheat the barbecue to medium-high. Using 2 Tbsp. (30 mL) of the olive oil, brush the eggplant slices on both sides. Grill each side, turning once, until golden brown and tender. (Or broil the eggplant in the oven on baking sheets until golden brown on both sides.) Let cool.

Toss the oyster mushrooms with the remaining 1 Tbsp. (15 mL) olive oil and 1/8 tsp. (.5 mL) salt. Place them in a single layer on the grill, pressing down lightly with a lifter. Grill until well marked; flip over and grill on the other side. Let cool. (The mushrooms can also be broiled. Heat a sturdy baking sheet under the broiler for 5 minutes before adding the mushrooms. Distribute the mushrooms over the baking sheet and press with a lifter. Broil, turning once to brown the other side.)

Cut the eggplant and mushrooms into 1/2-inch (1.2-cm) pieces. Combine with the olives, garlic, chili, thyme and salt and pepper. Mix gently.

Preheat the oven to 400°F (200°C). Lightly sprinkle a 12- x 17-inch
(30- x 43-cm) baking sheet with cornmeal. Roll the flatbread dough evenly
onto the baking sheet, pressing it into the corners. Spread the topping on
he dough in an even layer. Bake in the middle of the oven for 10–15 minutes,
until the crust is firm. Slip the flatbread from the pan directly onto the oven
rack and bake for 10–15 minutes longer until the bottom crust is golden
brown. Turn off the oven, open the door and let sit for 5 minutes before
serving.

Preserving Herbs

A great way to save leftover fresh herbs, such as
thyme, sage and rosemary, is to store them in sea
salt. Rarely do you use a whole bunch of herbs at
once, so here is what you can do to save them.
Purchase high-quality coarse French sea salt,
available in specialty shops or health food stores.
Layer the fresh herb sprigs with the salt in small
glass jars. The flavour will be well preserved and
you can simply lift out and use the herbs as you
need them. When using dried herbs, use about
half the volume of fresh herbs called for in
recipes. The salt left in the jar becomes herbed
salt and can be used up wherever you want a
nice herbal undertone.

—Margaret Chisholm

Springtime Open-Face Asparagus Sandwich

I have served a version of this dish as an appetizer for a spring dinner party at least once a year for years. Buy the fattest asparagus you can find, splurge on some special extra virgin olive oil, break the piggy bank for a nice chunk of Parmigiano-Reggiano and drive across town to get the finest sourdough. You only have to plan ahead to make the oven-dried cherry tomatoes. These little gems are sweet, salty and tangy and can be used in many ways. Toss them in pasta dishes, serve them with grilled Provençal garlic shrimp, use them as a garnish or add them to a sandwich. They keep nicely for a day wrapped on a plate at room temperature. If you don't have time to make the dried cherry tomatoes, simply use fresh ones.

Serves 4		Margaret Chisholm
20	cherry tomatoes	20
	coarse sea salt to taste	
1 Tbsp.	balsamic vinegar	15 mL
5 Tbsp.	extra virgin olive oil	75 mL
	salt and freshly ground black pepper to taste	
20	pieces asparagus	20
4	thick slices sourdough bread	4
1	clove garlic, cut in half	1
4 oz.	Parmigiano-Reggiano shavings	115 g
	salt and freshly ground black pepper to taste	

Cut the cherry tomatoes in half horizontally and place cut side up on a baking sheet. Sprinkle with coarse sea salt. Bake at 275°F (135°C) for 1 hour and 15 minutes. They should be somewhat dried out, but still a little moist and chewy in the centre.

Whisk together the balsamic vinegar and 3 Tbsp. (45 mL) of the olive oil. Season well with salt and pepper. Set aside.

Cut the tough ends off the bottom of the asparagus and peel the bottom half with a sharp peeler. Place the asparagus on a plate, drizzle with 1 Tbsp. (15 mL) of the olive oil and sprinkle with salt and pepper. Toss to coat evenly. Grill the asparagus on a preheated barbecue or cast-iron grill for 3–4 minutes or until softened slightly. Remove from the heat and keep warm.

While the asparagus is grilling, toast the sourdough slices under the broiler on both sides. Rub each slice of toast with the cut side of the garlic clove. Drizzle with the remaining olive oil.

Arrange a piece of garlic toast on each of 4 plates. Top each slice with 5 pieces of asparagus and generous shavings of cheese. Sprinkle the cherry tomatoes around the plate. Drizzle with the dressing.

● ● ● ● ● ●
Quick Fix:

Cambozola and Wine Jelly Canapés

Girl Guides taught me to always be prepared. If you keep a supply of bread and your favourite cheese and jelly on hand at all times, you will be prepared for any entertaining emergencies. As head baker of Terra Breads, it goes without saying that I always have bread on hand. One of my favourite cheeses is Cambozola, a cross between Brie and blue cheese. Wine jelly is sold at specialty stores. To make the canapés, slice the bread into bite-size pieces and spread each piece with some cheese and a dollop of wine jelly. Serve immediately to unexpected hungry guests while you go order a pizza!

—Mary Mackay

Crispy Saint André and Leek Wedges

Imagine a thin-crust pizza that's gone uptown. It's crisp and buttery on the bottom with a thin layer of tangy cheese and soft sweet leeks— a perfect invitation to a chilled glass of wine. Don't panic if the crust shrinks; the leeks hold the filling in place nicely while baking. A few cooked asparagus spears chopped into the mix are tasty as well.

Makes one 11- x 17-inch (28- x 43-cm) tart		*Glenys Morgan*
1 cup	unsalted butter, chilled	240 mL
2 1/2 cups	flour	600 mL
1/2 tsp.	salt	2.5 mL
1/2 cup	water	120 mL
6–8	leeks trimmed to include 2 inches (5 cm) of light green end	6–8
4 Tbsp.	unsalted butter	60 mL
4 Tbsp.	white wine or water	60 mL
	salt and freshly ground white pepper to taste	
2	large eggs	2
2	egg yolks	2
1 cup	whipping cream	240 mL
1/2 tsp.	curry powder (optional)	2.5 mL
2 Tbsp.	Dijon mustard	30 mL
6–8 oz.	Saint André (rind removed), chèvre, bleu or any creamy cheese	170–227 g
1 Tbsp.	thyme leaves	15 mL

Cut the 1 cup (240 mL) butter into 1/2-inch (1.2-cm) pieces. Combine the flour and salt. Add the butter pieces to the flour and blend, using a pastry blender or your finger and thumb to flatten the butter into pieces like large oatmeal flakes. Add the water and gather the dough into a ball. Wrap it in plastic wrap, using enough to wrap generously around the dough. For easy rolling, flatten the dough inside the plastic wrap into an elongated rectangle approximately 1 inch (2.5 cm) thick. Chill for 30 minutes or longer before rolling.

Let the dough warm enough to roll without cracking. Roll to 1/8 inch (.3 cm) thickness and fit it into an 11- x 17-inch (28- x 43-cm) baking sheet. Prick the dough with a fork until it resembles a cracker. Trim the edges and chill for at least 30 minutes, or preferably freeze, before baking. The tiny holes and chilling prevent shrinking. Bake directly from the refrigerator or freezer.

Preheat the oven to 400°F (200°C). Bake the crust until golden on the edges and the centre appears dry, about 10–15 minutes. This step creates the crispy crust and sets the shape. Make the crust up to 2 days ahead to this point or prepare the topping while it's baking.

For the topping, cut the leeks in half lengthwise and slice diagonally into thin slices. Rinse the leeks to remove any dirt, drain and pat dry. In a skillet with a lid, melt the butter and add the leeks and wine or water. Season with salt and pepper. Stir to coat the leeks. Reduce the heat, cover and braise the leeks until they're tender. Remove the cover to allow the liquid to evaporate. Set aside until needed.

Whisk together the eggs, egg yolks and cream. Add the curry powder, if desired, to complement milder cheeses. Brush the partially baked crust with Dijon mustard. Spread the leeks evenly over the crust and dot small pieces of the cheese over the mixture. Pour the egg and cream mixture over the leeks and sprinkle with the fresh thyme. Return to the oven and bake until the centre is firm and the edges are golden, about 20 minutes. Let it rest for 5 minutes before cutting.

Serving Cheese

Always have cheese at room temperature for at least 2 hours prior to serving to allow its full flavour to come out.

—Lesley Stowe

Roasted Red Onion and Shallot Tart with Thyme

This dish raises the profile of the humble onion to new heights.
You could use Walla Walla or Maui onions but I really love the look of
red onion on this tart. You can also make this as individual tartlets.
Serve it with the Salad of Bitter Greens with Walnut Dressing
(The Girls Who Dish, page 32) as a first course or a light luncheon.

Serves 8		Lesley Stowe
5	medium red onions	5
12	large shallots, peeled	12
2–3 Tbsp.	extra virgin olive oil	30–45 mL
4 Tbsp.	balsamic vinegar	60 mL
	salt and freshly ground black pepper to taste	
2	white onions	2
4 Tbsp.	extra virgin olive oil	60 mL
1 Tbsp.	sugar	15 mL
2 tsp.	Dijon mustard	10 mL
2 Tbsp.	heavy cream	30 mL
8 oz.	frozen puff pastry	227 g
2 tsp.	fresh thyme	10 mL
	salt and freshly ground black pepper to taste	

Preheat the oven to 375°F (190°C). Cut the red onions into eighths lengthwise. Cut the shallots in half lengthwise. Drizzle two large baking sheets with the 2–3 Tbsp. (30–45 mL) oil and spread the onions and shallots on the sheets, keeping the wedges intact. Sprinkle with balsamic vinegar, salt and pepper. Cover with foil and roast for 20 minutes. Uncover and roast an additional 15–20 minutes until golden and tender. Let cool.

Cut the white onions in half lengthwise. Cutting with the grain, slice the onion into 1/4-inch (.6-cm) pieces. Heat the 4 Tbsp. (60 mL) oil in a heavy sauté pan, add the onion and cook over medium-low heat until soft and golden brown, approximately 15 minutes. Sprinkle with the sugar and continue cooking until the onions are a deep golden brown. Add the Dijon mustard and cream. Set aside and let cool.

On a floured surface roll the puff pastry into a round. Using a 10-inch (25-cm) cake pan or a plate, cut out a circle and transfer it to a baking sheet. Prick the pastry with a fork and chill 10–15 minutes. Bake for 15 minutes. Remove from the oven, spread with the caramelized onions and arrange the onion wedges and shallots to cover the pastry. Sprinkle with thyme, salt and pepper. Bake approximately 15 minutes or until the pastry is puffed and golden. Serve warm.

Green Olives Baked with Sweet Sherry and Garlic

Warm olives are a different beast from cold ones. Plumply infused with garlic and sherry, they are sweet, salty and seductive. Serve with a bowl of roasted almonds and Roasted Garlic and Chive Crackers (page 2).

Serves 4		Karen Barnaby
1 cup	green, unpitted olives	240 mL
1/2 cup	sweet sherry	120 mL
1/4 tsp.	fennel seeds	1.2 mL
1/4 tsp.	coriander seeds	1.2 mL
2	cloves garlic, thinly sliced	2
2 tsp.	extra virgin olive oil	10 mL

Preheat the oven to 350°F (175°C). Combine all ingredients in a baking dish that will hold the olives snugly in a single layer. Bake uncovered for 20 minutes and serve warm.

Corn Blini with Smoked Salmon and Wasabi Cream

A little artistic license and the delicious duo of salmon and corn becomes an easy and elegant starter. Keep it simple or dress up the presentation by stacking a stylish layered tower of blini and salmon, topped with a cloud of wasabi cream and long thin chives. Don't worry about having extra wasabi powder—it's great in mashed potatoes or mixed with soy sauce and maple syrup and drizzled over salmon.

Tobiko is a bright orange, finely grained roe that makes a nice complement to salmon. It's available in Japanese markets and at most fish vendors that carry caviar or sushi supplies. Unused portions may be kept frozen for later use.

Makes 6 to 8 servings		*Glenys Morgan*
1 cup	sweet corn kernels (use canned or tiny frozen corn)	240 mL
4	large eggs	4
1/3 cup	flour	80 mL
1 1/2 cups	whipping cream	360 mL
1/2 tsp.	salt	2.5 mL
	freshly ground white pepper to taste	
2 Tbsp.	finely minced chives and dill	30 mL
1 tsp.	wasabi powder	5 mL
2 Tbsp.	finely minced chives, dill, chervil, tarragon or a blend	30 mL
4 Tbsp.	melted butter	60 mL
12–16	slices smoked salmon, lox-sliced	12–16
	fresh herb sprigs for garnish	
2 tsp.	tobiko or red caviar for garnish (optional)	10 mL

Purée the corn in the food processor or blender. Add the eggs, flour, 1/2 cup (125 mL) of the whipping cream, salt, pepper and 2 Tbsp. (30 mL) minced chives and dill. Blend well and set aside to rest for 20 minutes before using.

Blend a small amount of the remaining 1 cup (240 mL) whipping cream with the wasabi to wet the powder. Whisk the wasabi paste back into the whipping cream and continue to whip until firm peaks form. Fold in the remaining 2 Tbsp. (30 mL) minced herbs. Chill until ready to serve. For very finely minced herbs, whiz them together in a blender with half of the whipping cream, add to the remaining cream, then whip.

To cook the blini, melt enough butter to coat the skillet (a non-stick skillet may require less). Using a ladle, drop the corn batter in to create small cakes about 2–3 inches (5–7.5 cm) across. Turn the cakes when golden brown edges have formed and dry bubbles appear on top. Repeat in batches, adding more butter as needed. Hold the blini in a warm oven until you're ready to assemble and serve them.

To serve, arrange 3–4 warm blini in a circle with the edges overlapping. Top each piece with smoked salmon, shaping or rolling the salmon to fit on each blini. Add a dollop of the whipped wasabi herb cream to the centre of the plate. Garnish with herb sprigs. For a special touch, add a bit of caviar as well.

Optional: Sour cream may be substituted for the whipping cream for a sauce that can be drizzled on or added as a dollop in the centre. Low-fat sour cream may be used since it's not cooked. Refrigerate after blending to allow the sour cream to thicken.

Storing Parsley

To store parsley, wash the bunch in cold water and spin it dry. Pluck the tiny clusters of leaves with a bit of the tiny stem from each larger stem and place them in a plastic container. Poke holes in the lid, cover and store in the fridge. The parsley will last at least 2 weeks and up to 4, and it will be ready to use whenever you need it.

—Karen Barnaby

Chèvre and Pear Quesadillas with Cilantro Crema

*One day at the catering company we were in a hurry to create some
"breakfast hors d'oeuvres." We worked together to create these
quesadillas. They became an instant hit and we have been making them
by the hundreds ever since. We love this particular fruit and cheese
combination. While we were thinking about breakfast at the time, they
are good served any time of day.*

Makes 24 quesadillas		Margaret Chisholm
2	pears, peeled	2
1 Tbsp.	olive oil	15 mL
	salt and freshly ground black pepper to taste	
10 oz.	soft goat's cheese, crumbled	285 g
5 oz.	Monterey Jack cheese, grated	140 g
1	green onion, sliced	1
6	10-inch (25-cm) soft flour tortillas	6
1 recipe	Cilantro Crema	1 recipe

Cut the pears in half and remove the core with a melon baller. Cut into
1/3-inch-thick (.8-cm) slices. Toss with the olive oil and a little salt and
pepper. Grill or sauté for 1 minute on each side.

Chop the pears into 1/2-inch (1.2-cm) pieces. Combine the pear, cheeses and
green onion in a bowl and mix well. Divide the mixture into 6 portions and
spread 1 portion onto half of each tortilla. Fold the tortilla in half.

Heat a non-stick or cast-iron pan over medium heat. Cook each tortilla for
about 1 minute per side, or until the cheese melts. Cut each tortilla into 4
pieces. Serve with Cilantro Crema or your favourite fruit salsa.

Cilantro Crema

Makes 1 1/4 cups (300 mL)

1/2 cup	yogurt	120 mL
1/2 cup	mayonnaise	120 mL
1/2 tsp.	sugar	2.5 mL
1/4 tsp.	salt	1.2 mL
1 tsp.	ground cumin	5 mL
1 cup	finely chopped cilantro leaves	240 mL
1 tsp.	freshly squeezed lime juice	5 mL

Whisk everything together and chill.

Secret

In an emergency I race around my Gourmet Warehouse and pick up all the wonderful prepared foods— sauces, roasted peppers, marinated artichokes, olives, aged balsamics. I put together an elaborate, tasty antipasto tray, never telling the truth—condiments can make a great meal.

—Caren McSherry-Valagao

Gnocchi with Walnut Pesto

Forget those rubbery little nuggets that come out of the supermarket freezer. Made properly, these gnocchi are tender and light as clouds. Use mature white-skinned potatoes for best results. These gnocchi are also delicious with a light tomato sauce or basil pesto. The walnut pesto is a little rich, so this is best served as an appetizer.

Serves 4 as an appetizer		Margaret Chisholm
1 1/2 lbs.	white-skinned boiling or baking potatoes	680 g
1 1/2 cups	all-purpose flour	360 mL
3/4 tsp.	salt	4 mL
1 Tbsp.	coarse salt	15 mL
1 recipe	Walnut Pesto	1 recipe

Boil the potatoes in their skins in a large pot of water until tender. Drain. When cool enough to handle, peel the potatoes and put them through a potato ricer or grate them. Add the flour and 3/4 tsp. (4 mL) salt and stir until well combined. Place the mixture on a well-floured countertop and knead for 30 seconds. Flatten the dough out to a 1-inch (2.5-cm) slab. Cut it into 1-inch (2.5-cm) strips. Roll each strip into a rope and cut it into 1-inch (2.5-cm) pieces. Place on a well-floured cookie sheet.

Bring a large pot of water to a boil on high heat and add the coarse salt. Add the gnocchi and stir very gently. Boil the gnocchi until they rise to the top of the pot. Count to ten, then remove the gnocchi with a large slotted spoon and place them in a large bowl. Reserve 3/4 cup (180 mL) of the cooking water.

Mix the reserved cooking water with the walnut pesto. Add the gnocchi and toss well.

Spice Grinder

Purchase an extra coffee grinder for grinding spices

—Mary Mackay

Walnut Pesto

It is imperative to use fresh walnuts in the sauce, so purchase them at a busy health food store or specialty nut shop, or, even better, shell your own. Try walnut pesto on spaghetti or other thin pasta. Remember to always loosen the pesto with some pasta cooking water.

Makes 1 cup (240 mL)

1/2 cup	walnuts	120 mL
1/2 cup	parsley, preferably flat-leaf Italian, packed lightly	120 mL
1/4 cup	extra virgin olive oil	60 mL
2	cloves garlic, chopped	2
1 tsp.	lemon juice	5 mL
1/4 cup	freshly grated Parmesan cheese	60 mL
1/4 cup	freshly grated pecorino Romano cheese	60 mL

Place the walnuts, parsley, olive oil, garlic and lemon juice in a food processor. Process to a crumbly paste. Scrape down the sides of the bowl and process a few more seconds. Transfer to a bowl and mix in the cheeses by hand.

Rice Paper Stuffed with Purple Peruvian Potatoes

This sounds technical but it is as easy as mashing potatoes. The purple potatoes provide the wow factor, but if you can't find them, Yukon Golds are just as tasty. You can make them small for appetizers or larger for a first course. Don't skip the confit, it makes this recipe a standout.

Makes 18 to 24		*Caren McSherry-Valagao*
6	large purple Peruvian potatoes	6
4 Tbsp.	olive oil	60 mL
1	large yellow onion, diced	1
2–3	cloves garlic, minced	2–3
1/2 cup	oil-packed sun-dried tomatoes, chopped	120 mL
2 Tbsp.	creamed horseradish	30 mL
	sea salt and freshly ground black pepper to taste	
1	package 6-inch (15-cm) rice paper wrappers	1
1 recipe	Onion, Port and Balsamic Confit	1 recipe

Peel and boil the potatoes until they are tender, drain well and put them through a ricer. Set aside. Heat 2 Tbsp. (30 mL) of the olive oil in a frying pan; add the onion and garlic, and fry over medium heat until golden brown. Stir in the sun-dried tomatoes. Set aside.

Mix the riced potatoes, onion mixture and horseradish together. Taste for seasoning and adjust with salt and pepper.

Soak the rice papers in warm water until they become pliable, about 2–3 minutes. Place the rice paper on a kitchen towel to absorb some of the water. Take about 4 Tbsp. (60 mL) of the potato mixture and place it on the bottom edge of one soaked rice paper. Fold the sides of the rice paper over the potato and roll it up from the bottom, like an egg roll. Repeat with the remaining potato.

Heat a non-stick pan to medium-high, pour in about 1 Tbsp. (15 mL) of the remaining olive oil and fry the rolls on all sides until they are crisp and golden. Fry the rolls in batches, adding more oil if required. Serve with the confit.

Onion, Port and Balsamic Confit

This condiment is good enough to bottle and sell. Don't be alarmed at the number of onions called for in the recipe, they will cook down to half. This keeps very well refrigerated—that is, if it is not eaten on the first offering. It is great with any grilled meat or poultry. Stand back and wait for the applause.

Makes 3 1/2 cups (840 mL)

8	medium yellow or white onions	8
4 Tbsp.	good olive oil	60 mL
1/4 cup	balsamic vinegar	60 mL
1/4 cup	port	60 mL
2/3 cup	brown sugar	160 mL
	freshly ground black pepper to taste	

Slice the onions as thin as possible. Heat the olive oil in a large sauté pan, add the onions and sauté on medium heat for about 15–20 minutes, stirring occasionally. If the onions begin to stick, cover the pan to create a little moisture.

When the onions are a dark caramel brown, add the vinegar, port and sugar. Cook an additional 15 minutes, or until the mixture is the consistency of marmalade. Adjust the seasoning with pepper.

Pepper Shooters

I tasted my first stuffed cherry pepper with my husband John, a passionate pepper lover, during a memorable trip to the Napa Valley in California—memorable not just for the great food and wine, but because John proposed on this trip. I came across the fresh peppers in our local market at the end of the summer and pickled them for winter use. If pickling is not your thing, you can find jars of pickled sweet cherry peppers in supermarkets. If you like it hot, try stuffing pickled jalapeño or pepperoncini peppers instead. The peppers come in a variety of sizes; look for small bite-size ones. These are a fun appetizer and perfect to bring along on a picnic with lots of bread and wine.

Makes 2 dozen		Mary Mackay
24	pickled sweet cherry peppers, tops removed	24
24	small leaves fresh basil	24
3 oz.	provolone cheese, cut into 24 3/4-inch (2-cm) cubes	85 g
12	very thin slices prosciutto, cut in half	12
2 Tbsp.	olive oil	30 mL

Scoop the seeds out of the cherry peppers with a small melon baller or teaspoon and discard. Run the peppers under water to rinse out extra seeds and place them upside down on paper towel to drain.

Place one basil leaf on top of each cube of provolone, then wrap a slice of prosciutto around each cube. Stuff the cherry peppers with the prosciutto and provolone packages. Place the stuffed peppers in a bowl and gently toss with the olive oil.

The peppers can be stored in the fridge in a plastic container for your picnic or transferred to a serving dish for immediate consumption.

Salt Cod "Seviche"

While cooked salt cod can be dry, preparing it as a seviche preserves all of its succulence. Salt cod requires a bit of planning ahead as it has to be soaked overnight, but don't let that deter you. I find this to be more delicious than regular seviche. Serve it with good bread and a bowl of olives.

Serves 4		Karen Barnaby
1/2 lb.	boneless, skinless salt cod	227 g
2 Tbsp.	extra virgin olive oil	30 mL
2	cloves garlic, peeled and lightly crushed	2
2 Tbsp.	finely chopped onion	30 mL
1 Tbsp.	lime juice	15 mL
2	ripe tomatoes, peeled, seeded and chopped to a pulp	2
1/4 cup	coarsely chopped cilantro leaves	60 mL
1	small hot chili, finely chopped	1
	freshly ground black pepper to taste	

Soak the salt cod in water for up to 2 days, changing the water frequently.

Tear the cod into a few pieces, then tear each piece into small shreds. Do not use a knife. I use a fork to shred the cod by dragging the tines with the grain. Press out the water with your hands. Place the cod in a bowl and add the olive oil and garlic. Toss well and refrigerate.

Combine the onion with the lime juice and let sit for 30 minutes. Add the lime juice, onion and chopped tomato to the cod. Mix well. Refrigerate until serving time.

Just before serving, remove the garlic. Add the cilantro, chili and black pepper. Mix well and serve.

Crab and Shrimp Potstickers with Dipping Sauce

We eat these by the dozen. You can find the gyoza wrappers at specialty stores or Asian markets. This is another do-ahead appetizer— make the potstickers ahead and refrigerate or freeze them until cooking time.

Makes 24 potstickers		Deb Connors
4 oz.	crabmeat	113 g
4 oz.	shrimp	113 g
1/2 cup	sliced shiitake mushrooms	120 mL
3 Tbsp.	finely grated carrot	45 mL
2	green onions, chopped	2
2	cloves garlic, chopped	2
2 tsp.	sweet chili sauce	10 mL
1/2 tsp.	salt	2.5 mL
1/4 tsp.	freshly ground black pepper	1.2 mL
24	gyoza wrappers	24
1 Tbsp.	vegetable oil	15 mL
1/2 cup	chicken stock	120 mL
1 recipe	Dipping Sauce	1 recipe

To prepare the filling, combine the crabmeat and shrimp in a small bowl and mix well. Add the mushrooms, carrot, green onion, garlic and sweet chili sauce. Mix well and season with salt and pepper.

Lay a wrapper on a work surface and place 1 heaping tsp. (5–7 mL) of filling in the centre. Moisten the edges of the wrapper with water. Bring the sides of the wrapper up around the filling to a point at the top, pleating the sides and pressing at the top to seal it closed. Repeat with the remaining wrappers and filling.

Heat the oil in a large non-stick sauté pan over high heat until it's very hot. Place the potstickers in the pan, taking care not to overcrowd them. Cook for 2 minutes, until they start to brown. Carefully add the chicken stock, cover the pan, reduce the heat to low and steam for 2 minutes. Remove the potstickers from the pan and serve with the dipping sauce.

Dipping Sauce

Makes about 1/2 cup (120 mL)

1	clove garlic, chopped	1
1 tsp.	peeled and chopped ginger	5 mL
1 Tbsp.	honey	15 mL
1	lime, juice only	1
1 tsp.	sweet chili sauce	5 mL
1 Tbsp.	soy sauce	15 mL
1/2 cup	chicken stock	120 mL
1 tsp.	cornstarch	5 mL
1 tsp.	cold water	5 mL

Combine all the ingredients except the cornstarch and water in a small saucepan and bring to a simmer. Combine the cornstarch and water and whisk it into the sauce. Cook until the sauce is clear, about 3 minutes. Remove from the heat and set aside until you're ready to use it.

• • • • • •

Quick Fix:

Better than Nachos

No one can cook from an empty cupboard and everyone's staples are different. A favourite snack I make requires 5 or 6 basics, depending on my mood. It's low in fat and big on flavour.

- Rosarita vegetarian refried beans (canned)
- Que Pasa flour tortillas (fresh or in the freezer)
- log of chèvre (keeps 3 months unopened)
- chipotles in adobo sauce (lasts for ages refrigerated or can be frozen)
- sour cream or yogurt
- salsa

Spread one tortilla with beans and another with chèvre. Put the tortillas together with the goodies inside. Purée one or two chipotles with some sour cream or yogurt. Grill the quesadillas in a hot pan or microwave. (I like the toasty flavour from my pancake griddle.) Cut into wedges and serve with the chipotle cream and salsa to dip the wedges into.

—Glenys Morgan

Crab Cakes with Watercress and Roast Curry Vinaigrette

This is a very easy do-ahead dish that will impress the fussiest of guests. The crab cakes can easily be made a day ahead, the vinaigrette, two to three days. Keep refrigerated and bring it to room temperature before serving. The roast curry vinaigrette is mild but full of flavour.

Serves 4		Deb Connors
1	egg, beaten	1
2 Tbsp.	good-quality mayonnaise	30 mL
1 tsp.	Worcestershire sauce	5 mL
1/2 tsp.	hot pepper sauce	2.5 mL
1 Tbsp.	fresh lemon juice	15 mL
1 tsp.	Dijon mustard	5 mL
1 lb.	fresh Dungeness crabmeat	454 g
1/4 tsp.	black pepper	1.2 mL
1/4 tsp.	curry powder	1.2 mL
1 cup	fresh bread crumbs	240 mL
3 Tbsp.	celery, finely diced	45 mL
3 Tbsp.	red pepper, seeds and membrane removed, finely diced	45 mL
3 Tbsp.	yellow pepper, seeds and membrane removed, finely diced	45 mL
2 Tbsp.	red onion, finely diced	30 mL
3 Tbsp.	canola oil	45 mL
1 recipe	Roast Curry Vinaigrette	1 recipe
4	sprigs watercress	4

Combine the egg, mayonnaise, Worcestershire sauce, hot pepper sauce, lemon juice and Dijon mustard; stir well. Squeeze the excess moisture out of the crabmeat, and add it to the mixture. Add the black pepper, curry powder and bread crumbs; mix it well by hand. Mix in the celery, red and yellow peppers and onion. The mixture should be firm enough to hold together.

Form the crab mixture into 8 patties of uniform size. Refrigerate for 1/2 hour to overnight.

Heat the canola oil in a large heavy sauté pan. Fry the crab cakes in two batches over medium-high heat for 3–4 minutes per side until golden. Drain on paper towel.

To serve, place 2 crab cakes overlapping in the centre of each of 4 small plates. Drizzle the vinaigrette over the crab cakes and a little on the plate. Garnish with a small bunch of watercress next to the crab cakes.

Roast Curry Vinaigrette

The vinaigrette may be prepared one day ahead. Bring it to room temperature before using.

Makes 3/4 cup (180 mL)

1 Tbsp.	olive oil	15 mL
2 Tbsp.	finely diced onion	30 mL
1	clove garlic, chopped	1
1	tomato, chopped	1
1 Tbsp.	curry powder	15 mL
1 tsp.	cumin	5 mL
1 tsp.	turmeric	5 mL
1 tsp.	chopped fresh thyme	5 mL
1 tsp.	chopped fresh parsley	5 mL
2	bay leaves	2
3 Tbsp.	white wine	45 mL
1/4 cup	chicken stock	60 mL
2 Tbsp.	white wine vinegar	30 mL
1 Tbsp.	fresh lime juice	15 mL
1/2 cup	olive oil	120 mL
	salt and freshly ground black pepper to taste	

Heat the 1 Tbsp. (15 mL) olive oil in a sauté pan over medium-high heat. Add the onion, garlic, tomato, curry powder, cumin and turmeric and sauté for 2 minutes. Add the thyme, parsley and bay leaves, then the white wine and chicken stock. Reduce the heat and simmer until the liquid is reduced by half, 3–4 minutes. Discard the bay leaves. Place the mixture in a blender and with the machine running add the white wine vinegar and lime juice and slowly pour in the 1/2 cup (120 mL) olive oil. Adjust the seasoning with salt and pepper.

Spicy Jumbo Prawns with Nutty Herb Sauce

Memories of a taco stand in Mexico led to cravings for crispy prawns in a masa corn batter, and warm tortillas with thick cream and fresh herb salsa. This version keeps me happy and there's no frying! Smaller prawns are tasty, but the jumbo prawns balance the heat and add drama. Serve them with warmed or grilled flour tortillas or taco chips to scoop the rest of the sauce. The prawns on their own are delicious with a cooling fruit salsa such as Citrus Mango Relish (page 123).

Serves 4		Glenys Morgan
8	jumbo tiger prawns (8–12 count)	8
2 Tbsp.	olive oil	30 mL
2	chipotle chiles en adobo, minced	2
2 Tbsp.	dark brown sugar	30 mL
1/4 tsp.	salt	1.2 mL
1 cup	hulled unroasted pumpkin seeds, about 4 oz. (113 g)	240 mL
1 cup	cilantro, loosely packed	240 mL
1	small white onion, peeled and coarsely chopped	1
1 cup	chicken stock	240 mL
1 Tbsp.	butter	15 mL
1 cup	sour cream	240 mL
	salt to taste	
1 Tbsp.	olive oil	15 mL
	cilantro sprigs for garnish	

Prepare the prawns by removing the shells down to the last tail section, leaving the tail to hold on to while nibbling. On the outside or back of the prawn, use a sharp paring knife to score down to the vein and remove it. The scoring allows the prawn to curl when cooked.

Blend together the 2 Tbsp. (30 mL) olive oil, minced chipotle chiles, brown sugar and salt. Add the prawns and toss to coat with the sauce. They can be cooked immediately, but for a hotter, smokier version, marinate for several hours.

Toast the pumpkin seeds in a dry heavy skillet until lightly browned. Purée the seeds, cilantro, onion and chicken stock in a blender until smooth. Heat the butter in a skillet and add the purée. Warm through and add the sour cream. Scrape the bottom of the pan to incorporate the ingredients and prevent burning, and season with salt. Cook the sauce over gentle heat until it's bubbling and hot. Keep it warm until it's needed.

Use the remaining olive oil to coat the barbecue grill or skillet; either should be searing hot. Cook the prawns until they are pink and opaque. Remove from the heat and keep warm. Spoon the warm sauce onto each plate and stand the prawns with tails up in the sauce. Garnish with cilantro sprigs and serve immediately.

Simple Abundance

Simple abundance is the rule many caterers use to dazzle partygoers at the table. Guests always gasp when they see a basket filled with perfect strawberries. Grill not one bunch but several when asparagus is in season and serve them simply with a dipping sauce. Instead of serving several tiny prawns as an appetizer, choose two jumbo prawns perfectly cooked and beautifully sauced for drama. Large tomatoes sliced lose their glory compared to cupfuls of tiny cherry tomatoes combined with large leaves of basil for a salad.

—Glenys Morgan

Prawn Spring Rolls with Lime Cilantro Dipping Sauce

Serve these as an appetizer at your next cocktail party. They're wonderful with champagne and easily done ahead. They are also nice as a garnish for a small salad. You can buy the wrappers in the freezer section at Asian supermarkets and other specialty stores. These spring rolls freeze well, so double the recipe and have them on hand for another occasion.

Makes 8 spring rolls		Deb Connors
8 oz.	prawns, shelled and deveined, cut into 1/2 inch (1.2-cm) pieces	227 g
1/2	lemon, juiced, and zest, chopped	1/2
2 tsp.	chopped cilantro	10 mL
1 Tbsp.	peeled and chopped ginger	15 mL
2	cloves garlic, chopped	2
	pinch dried chilies	
2 tsp.	oyster sauce	10 mL
2 tsp.	soy sauce	10 mL
1 tsp.	sweet chili sauce	5 mL
3	green onions, thinly sliced on the diagonal	3
1/4 cup	carrot, cut into fine julienne	60 mL
1/2	red bell pepper, cut into fine julienne	1/2
1/4 tsp.	salt	1.2 mL
1/4 tsp.	freshly ground black pepper	1.2 mL
8	8- x 8-inch (20- x 20-cm) spring roll wrappers	8
1 Tbsp.	all-purpose flour	15 mL
1 Tbsp.	water	15 mL
2 cups	oil	475 mL
1 recipe	Lime Cilantro Dipping Sauce	1 recipe
8	sprigs cilantro	8

In a bowl, combine the prawns, lemon zest and juice, cilantro, ginger, garlic, chilies, oyster sauce, soy sauce, sweet chili sauce, green onion, carrot and red pepper. Season with salt and pepper.

Separate the spring roll wrappers by peeling back a corner and pulling firmly but gently until the sheet is free. In a small bowl mix the flour and water to form a thin paste. Divide the prawn mixture into 8 equal portions. With one corner facing you so that the wrapper has a diamond shape, place one portion of the prawn mixture 1/3 of the way up the wrapper. Arrange the filling in a cigar shape. Fold the bottom point of the wrapper over the mixture, fold over the two sides and roll it up tightly until you come to the opposite corner. Dab this corner with a little of the flour paste mixture and seal. Continue until you have rolled 8 spring rolls. These can be frozen at this point.

Heat the oil in a heavy saucepan or deep fryer. When the oil has reached 350°F (175°C), place the spring rolls in the oil. Do not overcrowd. Cook for 3–4 minutes, or 6–7 minutes if they have been frozen. Set the spring rolls on paper towel to drain and cool before cutting.

To serve, cut each spring roll on the diagonal. Arrange the pieces on 4 small plates or 1 large one. Serve the dipping sauce in a small bowl on the side or drizzle it over the spring rolls and spoon some of the finely diced vegetables on the plate. Garnish with sprigs of cilantro.

Lime Cilantro Dipping Sauce

Makes 3/4 cup (180 mL)

1/2	lime, juice only	1/2
2 tsp.	honey	10 mL
2 tsp.	Dijon mustard	10 mL
1 tsp.	chopped cilantro	5 mL
1/4 cup	rice wine vinegar	60 mL
1/2 cup	canola oil	120 mL
	salt and freshly cracked black pepper to taste	
1 Tbsp.	very finely diced red onion	15 mL
1 Tbsp.	very finely diced red pepper	15 mL
1 Tbsp.	very finely diced carrot	15 mL

In a small bowl combine the lime juice, honey, mustard and cilantro. Using a small whisk, add the rice wine vinegar. Still whisking, slowly drizzle in the oil. Season with salt and pepper. Stir in the onion, red pepper and carrot.

Tiger Mussels with Garlicky Focaccia Crumbs

Although it's hard to beat mussels steamed with white wine and shallots, a friend of mine who is crazy about mussels inspired me to come up with this recipe.

Serves 6 as a first course or 24 as an hors d'oeuvre		Lesley Stowe
1/3 cup	olive oil	80 mL
4	cloves garlic, minced	4
1 1/2 cups	dried focaccia bread crumbs	360 mL
2	Roma tomatoes, seeded and finely diced	2
1/2 cup	minced parsley	120 mL
	salt and freshly ground black pepper to taste	
6 dozen	mussels	6 dozen
1/4 cup	Pernod	60 mL
1 cup	dry white wine	240 mL
	lemon wedges for garnish	

Heat the olive oil in a sauté pan over low heat. Add the garlic and sauté until soft. Add the focaccia crumbs, tomato and parsley. Season with salt and pepper. Set aside.

Scrub the mussels under cold running water and beard them. Pour the Pernod and wine into a large pot. Add the mussels, cover and cook over high heat just until the mussel shells open, about 5 minutes. Remove from the heat and let cool until they are easy to handle.

Remove and discard the top shell from each mussel, as well as any mussels that haven't opened. Use a small knife to gently release the mussels from the shells, then nestle them back into the shells. The mussels may either be arranged on individual gratin dishes or in rows on a large baking sheet. Sprinkle the bread crumb mixture over each mussel to cover it completely. At this point the mussels can be refrigerated for up to 4 hours before baking.

When ready to cook, preheat the oven to 475°F (250°C). Bake the mussels until sizzling and golden brown, 5–7 minutes. Garnish with lemon wedges and serve immediately.

Smoky Mussels

I first tested this recipe on dinner guests without knowing the real power of dried chipotle peppers. I wanted it to taste smoky so I added a lot of dried chipotles. The dish was unbearably hot but everyone was polite and ate it anyway. I have since cut back on the chipotle. I grind the dried chipotles in a coffee grinder—not the one we use for coffee! Chipotle peppers are also available canned in adobo sauce. Just rinse off the sauce and use a little more as they are not as strong as the dried peppers. If you would like this dish to be extra smoky, add a drop of liquid smoke or a dash of smoked paprika. Both are available in specialty stores.

Serves 4		Mary Mackay
2	slices double-smoked bacon, diced	2
1/3 cup	diced leeks, white part only	80 mL
1/3 cup	diced red bell pepper	80 mL
1 Tbsp.	minced garlic	15 mL
1/2 tsp.	ground dried chipotle peppers	2.5 mL
1 1/4 cups	dry white wine	300 mL
32	fresh mussels, washed and debearded	32
1/4 cup	heavy cream	60 mL
4 tsp.	chopped cilantro	20 mL

Heat a large saucepan on medium heat. Add the bacon and sauté until almost crisp. Stir in the leeks and red pepper and cook for 4 minutes until the vegetables are lightly browned. Add the garlic and chipotle peppers and cook 1 minute longer.

Increase the temperature to medium-high, add the white wine and bring to a full boil. Stir in the mussels and heavy cream, cover with a lid and cook until the mussels open, 5–8 minutes. Transfer to heated bowls, top with cilantro and serve with bread for soaking up the sauce.

Indian Candy Cakes with Lemon Dill Aïoli

Crab cakes are an hors d'oeuvres staple from one coast to the next, but what could be more fitting here on the West Coast than a salmon cake? Indian candy-style salmon makes a cake like no other.

Makes 36		Caren McSherry-Valagao
1 lb.	Indian candy	454 g
1/3 cup	finely chopped green onion	80 mL
1/2 cup	finely diced green pepper	120 mL
1 Tbsp.	grainy Dijon mustard	15 mL
1/4 cup	finely chopped fresh parsley	60 mL
2 Tbsp.	prepared horseradish	30 mL
1 tsp.	piri piri sauce, or any hot sauce	5 mL
1	large egg, beaten	1
1/3 cup	good-quality whole-egg mayonnaise	80 mL
	sea salt and freshly ground black pepper to taste	
3/4 cup	fresh white bread crumbs	180 mL

Flake the salmon into a large mixing bowl, removing any visible bones. Add the onion, green pepper, mustard, parsley, horseradish, hot sauce, egg and mayonnaise. Mix well to combine, and season with salt and pepper. Stir in the bread crumbs, adding more if the mixture is too moist. Form into small patties.

Sauté the cakes over medium heat in a non-stick pan until they are golden brown, about 3 minutes on each side. Serve warm or at room temperature with the aïoli.

Parsley in a Glass

To keep parsley fresh I store it in the fridge in a glass with the stems immersed in an inch (2.5 cm) of water.

—Mary Mackay

Lemon Dill Aïoli

Makes 3/4 cup (180 mL)

3	cloves garlic, peeled	3
2 Tbsp.	fresh lemon juice	30 mL
1/4 cup	fresh dill sprigs	60 mL
1	egg yolk	1
3/4 cup	extra virgin olive oil	180 mL
	sea salt and freshly ground black pepper to taste	

Purée the garlic, lemon juice and dill in the bowl of a food processor. Add the egg yolk and pulse to mix. With the machine running, slowly pour the olive oil through the feed tube until a thick sauce is formed. Adjust the seasoning with salt and pepper.

Serve with the salmon cakes. If you omit the dill, you can use it wherever aïoli is called for.

Secret Craving

Crusty bread spread with truffle honey and thin slices of prosciutto di Parma make an intoxicating, addictive and positively ambrosial combination. Truffle honey is liquid honey that is infused with truffle essence, available at specialty food stores.

—Lesley Stowe

Soups

Roast Squash and Pear Soup

Substitute your favourite squash for the butternut, if you like. If you use a hard-to-peel squash such as acorn, simply cut the squash in half, scrape out the seeds, drop a pat of butter in each half and roast until soft. Let the squash cool a little and scrape out the pulp.

Serves 4		Deb Connors
2	butternut squash, peeled and diced, approximately 1 1/2 lbs. (680 g)	2
3 Tbsp.	olive oil	45 mL
1	onion, diced	1
1 tsp.	peeled and chopped ginger	5 mL
1/2 cup	dry sherry	120 mL
2	pears, peeled and diced	2
6 cups	chicken stock	1.5 L
1 cup	apple juice	240 mL
2	sprigs fresh thyme	2
1/4 tsp.	ground nutmeg	1.2 mL
1 cup	heavy cream	240 mL
	salt and freshly ground black pepper to taste	
	lemon juice to taste	
4	slices French bread, cut 1/2 inch (1.2 cm) thick	4
2 tsp.	olive oil	10 mL
4	thin slices Camembert cheese	4
1 Tbsp.	butter	15 mL
1	pear, peeled and cored, cut in small dice	1
1 Tbsp.	honey	15 mL
4	sprigs fresh thyme	4

Preheat the oven to 375°F (190°C). Place the diced squash in a roasting pan and drizzle with 2 Tbsp. (30 mL) of the olive oil. Roast until the squash is tender, about 40 minutes.

Heat the remaining 1 Tbsp. (15 mL) olive oil in a medium saucepan, add the onion and ginger and sauté until the onion is soft. Add the squash, the sherry and the pears. Pour in the chicken stock and apple juice. Add the 2 thyme sprigs and nutmeg. Bring to a boil and simmer for approximately 1/2 hour.

Remove the thyme sprigs, pour the soup into a blender and purée until very smooth. Return it to the saucepan and stir in the cream. Bring the soup to a simmer and cook for 10 minutes. Season with salt, pepper and lemon juice.

Preheat the oven to 375°F (190°C).

To make the croutons, brush the bread slices on both sides with olive oil and bake them on a cookie sheet for 5 minutes until lightly toasted. Remove and let cool. Place the Camembert slices on the bread. Heat the butter in a small sauté pan and add the diced pear and honey. Cook over medium heat until nicely glazed. Spoon the pears over the Camembert.

To serve, divide the soup into 4 bowls and place a crouton on top of each serving. Garnish the crouton with a sprig of fresh thyme.

Secret Craving

In the cold winter months, nothing spells comfort for me like a big steamy bowl of duck congee. Congee is a thin rice gruel that can be eaten plain or garnished with different savoury bits. Green onions, ginger, peanuts and crisp noodles are the most common, but I take the Thai approach and squeeze in fresh lime, fish sauce, chilies, fried garlic and cilantro. I usually make the rice part and buy a barbecued duck on my way home from work.

Another winter favourite is Lipton Chicken Noodle Soup with fat, succulent matzoh balls bobbing around in the bowl. With a side of processed cheese and some saltine crackers— heaven! Eating this makes me completely shed any food snobbery or notions of correctness I may have. And hey, everything comes from a package!

—Karen Barnaby

Butternut Squash and Fava Bean Soup with Truffle Oil

Fava beans have long been a favourite on Mediterranean menus and their popularity in North America is rapidly increasing. Take care when preparing them: they not only have a fuzzy thick outer pod, but once shelled you must remove the thin skin that covers the bean itself as it is very tough and quite unappetizing. The white truffle oil elevates this soup from pauper to prince. It's worth searching out in specialty food stores.

Serves 6 to 8		Caren McSherrry-Valagao
3 Tbsp.	good-quality olive oil	45 mL
1	large yellow cooking onion, diced	1
1	large carrot, diced	1
2	leeks, white part only, washed and sliced	2
2 lbs.	butternut squash, peeled, seeded and sliced	900 g
1	sweet potato, peeled and chopped	1
2 tsp.	chopped fresh sage	10 mL
8 cups	chicken stock	2 L
2 cups	green fava beans, frozen, fresh or canned	475 mL
1/2 cup	sour cream	120 mL
2 tsp.	white truffle oil	10 mL

Heat the oil in a large soup pot. Add the onion, carrot and leek. Cover and cook over medium heat for about 5–10 minutes, or until the vegetables are soft.

Add the squash, sweet potato and sage to the pot, cooking for an additional 5 minutes. Add the stock and bring to a boil. Turn down to a simmer and cook for 30 minutes.

In the bowl of a food processor, purée the soup in small batches, then return it to the pot. Add the fava beans to the soup and simmer until the soup and the beans are heated through. (If using fresh beans, blanch them before adding to the soup.) Ladle the soup into bowls and garnish with a dollop of sour cream and a generous sprinkle of truffle oil.

Roasted Garlic and Pumpkin Soup with Five-Spice Crèma

Pumpkin is a squash we often relegate to the dessert course, but the Italians have been using it in everything from soups to pasta for generations. The nutmeg and cinnamon add a depth and earthiness that make this soup a great comfort food for the fall.

Serves 8 to 10		Lesley Stowe
2	medium onions	2
2	large leeks	2
8 lbs.	pumpkin (preferably sugar pumpkin)	3.6 kg
6 Tbsp.	extra virgin olive oil	90 mL
8 cups	chicken stock	2 L
1/2 tsp.	nutmeg	2.5 mL
1	stick cinnamon	1
2	bulbs roasted garlic (approximately 30 cloves)	2
1 cup	cream	240 mL
	salt and freshly ground black pepper to taste	
	lemon juice to taste	
1 cup	crème fraîche (see page 165)	240 mL
1 tsp.	five-spice powder	5 mL

Roughly chop the onion and the white part of the leek. Peel, seed and chop the pumpkin into 1-inch (2.5-cm) cubes. Heat the olive oil in a 4- to 6-quart (4- to 5-L) stockpot. Sauté the onion and leek over medium-low heat for 10–15 minutes until soft. Add the pumpkin, stock, nutmeg and cinnamon stick. Squeeze the roasted garlic cloves out of their skins and into the stock mixture. Bring to a boil, reduce the heat and simmer until the vegetables are soft. Remove the cinnamon stick. Purée the mixture in 2-cup (475-mL) batches in a food processor until smooth. Return the mixture to the pot. Stir in the cream. Season with salt, pepper and lemon juice.

Mix together the crème fraîche and five-spice powder. Swirl 1 Tbsp. (15 mL) on the top of each bowl of soup and serve immediately.

Corn Chowder with Sage and White Cheddar

This quick soup is a creamy comfort food. The Southwestern combination of corn with sage is one of my favourites, but thyme and basil work just as well. For the right bite, the Cheddar must be extra old. For a great meal, serve with Quesadillas with Shrimp and Avocado Relish (The Girls Who Dish, page 8).

Serves 6 to 8		Glenys Morgan
1	large white onion	1
3	stalks celery	3
4 Tbsp.	unsalted butter	60 mL
2 cups	corn kernels (4–6 cobs or small frozen kernels)	475 mL
1	14-oz. (398-mL) can cream-style corn	1
2 cups	chicken or vegetable stock	475 mL
2 Tbsp.	fresh sage leaves, cut into fine strips	30 mL
	salt and freshly ground black pepper to taste	
2 Tbsp.	butter	30 mL
2 Tbsp.	flour	30 mL
1 cup	milk	240 mL
4 oz.	grated sharp white Cheddar cheese or crumbled feta cheese	113 g

Finely mince the onion and celery in the food processor or by hand. Their texture should be as fine as the corn kernels. In a Dutch oven or large saucepan, melt the 4 Tbsp. (60 mL) butter and sauté the onion and celery until soft and translucent. Keep the heat low to prevent cooking away the liquid and browning the vegetables.

Add the corn kernels, creamed corn, stock and sage. Bring to near boiling and simmer for 5 minutes. Season with salt and pepper.

While the soup is heating, melt the 2 Tbsp. (30 mL) butter in a small saucepan. Add the flour and cook gently for 2 minutes. Add the milk and whisk until incorporated. Cook until thickened to the consistency of cereal cream, then add it to the soup pot. The soup may be made ahead to this point.

Keep hot or reheat to a bare simmer. Just before serving, stir in the cheese until melted. Serve immediately.

Optional: For a fragrant flavour typical of Mexico, heat the milk with a cinnamon stick and some peppercorns before adding it to the roux. For a spicy version, sliver jalapeños into the soup or steep them in the milk.

Bone Stock

Roast chicken or veal bones to add flavour and colour to stocks. Preheat the oven to 400°F (200°C) and roast the bones, stirring occasionally, for 45 minutes. Add carrots, celery, onions and a small amount of tomato paste. Roast for another 30 minutes, deglaze with water, and proceed to make your stock as usual.

Freezing Stock

To save room in your freezer, reduce all stocks to 1/4 volume. This makes for intense, well-flavoured stocks. You can then add water or vegetable stock to increase the volume or use the reduced stock to add flavour to sauces and gravies. If you live where you can buy reduced stocks (glaces or demi-glaces) you can freeze them in ice-cube trays. When frozen, turn them out and store them in plastic bags in your freezer. This allows you to use the small amounts you would need to add flavour to sauces and soups.

—Deb Connors

Smoky Corn Chowder

Chowder takes on a brand-new personality with the addition of paprika. This is not just any paprika, but a smoked Spanish variety that transforms ordinary recipes into celebration foods. This method of smoking has been used in Spain for hundreds of years; by dry smoking the peppers the paprika assumes a flavour like no other. The paprika is available in specialty food stores. Try this soup and taste the distinctive difference smoked Spanish paprika lends it.

Serves 6 to 8		Caren McSherry-Valagao
10	slices pancetta (preferably the spicy variety), diced	10
1	large cooking onion, diced	1
3	stalks celery, diced	3
1	large leek, white part only, sliced	1
2 tsp.	smoked Spanish paprika	10 mL
6 cups	chicken stock	1 1/2 L
4	cobs of corn, kernels removed	4
1	large Idaho potato, peeled and diced	1
1/2 cup	chopped fresh parsley	120 mL
1	bulb roasted garlic	1
1 cup	cream or whole milk	240 mL
1/2 tsp.	piri piri sauce, or any hot sauce	2.5 mL
3	dashes Worcestershire sauce	3
	sea salt and freshly ground black pepper to taste	
4 Tbsp.	snipped fresh chives	60 mL

Place the pancetta in a large heavy pot and fry over medium-low heat until crispy. Add the onion, celery and leek and cook until soft. Stir in the smoked paprika and cook for about 2 more minutes.

Add the chicken stock, corn kernels, potato and parsley. Squeeze the garlic cloves from their skins into the pot. Simmer for about 30 minutes.

Add the cream, taking particular care not to boil the soup or it will curdle. Add the hot sauce, Worcestershire sauce, salt and pepper. Stir to combine, ensuring that at no time the mixture boils.

Ladle into soup bowls and garnish with snipped chives.

Caramelized Fennel and Leek Soup

Caramelizing the fennel adds a deep rich flavour to this soup.
Outrageously velvety, this sophisticated soup should head up your next
dinner party.

Serves 8 to 10		Lesley Stowe
4 Tbsp.	extra virgin olive oil	60 mL
6	stalks celery, sliced into 1/2-inch (1.2-cm) pieces	6
4	large leeks, white part only, rinsed and coarsely chopped	4
4	cloves garlic, sliced	4
4	bulbs fennel, trimmed and cut in half lengthwise	4
4 Tbsp.	unsalted butter	60 mL
1 Tbsp.	sugar	15 mL
10 cups	chicken stock	2.4 L
2	large potatoes, peeled and thinly sliced	2
1/2 cup	cream	120 mL
	juice of 1 lemon	
	salt and freshly ground black pepper to taste	
6	slices sourdough bread, cut 1 inch (2.5 cm) thick	6

Heat the oil in a 4- to 6-quart (4- to 6-L) stockpot. Sauté the celery, leeks and garlic over medium-low heat until the vegetables are soft, about 15 minutes. Remove the vegetables from the pot and set aside.

Cut the fennel into 1/4-inch (.6-cm) slices. Melt half the butter in a heavy sauté pan and add the fennel. Cook over medium-high heat until the fennel starts to brown. Turn to brown all sides. Sprinkle it with sugar to encourage the fennel to caramelize to a deep golden colour.

Turn up the heat and add the chicken stock. Whisk to scrape the caramelized bits off the bottom of the pot. Add the celery, leek, garlic and potatoes to the pot. Bring to a boil, reduce the heat and simmer 30 minutes. Purée the soup in 2-cup (475-mL) batches in a blender until smooth. Strain through a fine sieve. Return to the pot and stir in the cream and lemon juice. Season with salt and pepper.

Heat the grill or broiler and lightly grill the bread on both sides. Brush lightly with olive oil. Cut into 1-inch (2.5-cm) cubes. Scatter the bread on the hot soup and serve immediately.

Moroccan Tomato Soup

A tomato soup is like a blank canvas that can be painted with herbs and spices from around the world. It's a tasty way to learn. Here, spices used by Mexican cooks and in Indian curries are coaxed into a fragrant combination that colours it Morocco. The warmth of the toasted spices and a smoked Spanish paprika make this soup equally good hot or chilled with a swirl of yogurt for garnish.

Serves 6 to 12		*Glenys Morgan*
4 Tbsp.	olive oil	60 mL
2	large onions, very thinly sliced	2
1	bulb roasted garlic	1
1 Tbsp.	coriander seed	15 mL
2 Tbsp.	cumin seed	30 mL
1 tsp.	ground cinnamon	5 mL
1 Tbsp.	paprika, hot, sweet or smoked (available in specialty shops)	15 mL
2	28-oz. (796-mL) cans Italian plum tomatoes	2
2 cups	chicken or vegetable stock	475 mL
1 tsp.	salt	5 mL
	freshly ground black pepper to taste	
2	large oranges, zest and juice	2
2 Tbsp.	brown sugar (optional)	30 mL
1 bunch	fresh cilantro, minced	1 bunch

Heat the olive oil in a Dutch oven and gently brown the onions. As they release their juices, cover to sweat and soften their texture. Squeeze the garlic cloves from their skins and mix them into the onions.

In a small dry skillet over medium-high heat, toast the coriander and cumin seeds until fragrant. They may even pop. Grind them in a mortar and pestle or coffee grinder.

Add the toasted spices, cinnamon and paprika to the onions. Cook the spices for several minutes to develop a full flavour. Be careful not to burn the mixture or it will be bitter instead of sweet.

Drain the canned tomatoes and coarsely chop. Add the tomatoes and stock to the onions. Bring to a boil, reduce the heat and simmer for about 30 minutes. Near the end of the cooking time, zest and juice the oranges. Season the soup with salt and pepper, adding the orange juice and zest to brighten the flavour. Simmer for 5 minutes. If the soup needs a little sweetness, add the sugar to taste.

Cool the soup. Purée for a smooth texture and bright colour. The soup may be prepared ahead to this point and even frozen if desired. Reheat and taste for seasonings. Add fresh minced cilantro just before serving.

Minted Split Green Pea Soup

This vegetarian version of split pea soup is lightened up with mint. Trust me, you will not miss the ham hock! Some specialty stores sell smoked dried split peas, which would be perfect for this soup.

Serves 4 to 6		Mary Mackay
2 tsp.	vegetable oil	10 mL
1 1/3 cups	diced onion	320 mL
1 cup	diced carrot	240 mL
1/2 cup	diced leek, white part only	120 mL
1 Tbsp.	minced garlic	15 mL
2 1/2 cups	split green peas (check for stones)	600 mL
8 cups	vegetable stock or water	2 L
2 1/2 tsp.	sea salt	12.5 mL
1 Tbsp.	chopped parsley	15 mL
2 Tbsp.	chopped mint	30 mL
	freshly cracked black pepper to taste	

Heat the oil in a large soup pot over medium heat. Add the onion, carrot and leek and cook for 8 minutes, stirring often, until the vegetables are soft. Stir in the garlic and cook 1 minute longer. Add the split peas and vegetable stock and bring to a boil. Reduce the heat to low and simmer until the peas are soft, about 35 minutes.

Turn off the heat and stir in the salt, parsley and mint. Check the seasoning and adjust with more salt if needed. Season with pepper and serve in heated bowls.

Smoke and Lime Chicken Soup

*After tasting a chicken soup cooked over a charcoal fire in Mexico, I
tried to recreate the blend of flavours using fire-roasted jalapeños—
chipotles en adobo—a staple in my kitchen. Grilled chicken, roasted
garlic and browned onion added layers of flavours, but I still couldn't
get the citrus zing from ordinary limes. Kaffir lime leaves, Thai cooking
staples, were waiting in my freezer. Warmed in the broth, they provide
a delicious fresh lime flavour that rises above the smoke. Serve with a
wedge of cornbread and, for a cooling dessert, Pannacotta with Basil
and Cracked Black Pepper Strawberries (The Girls Who Dish,
page 151), just to keep things interesting.*

Serves 4 to 6		Glenys Morgan
1 tsp.	ground cumin	5 mL
2	cloves garlic, minced	2
2 tsp.	olive oil	10 mL
2	whole boneless skinless chicken breasts, halved	2
4 cups	chicken stock	950 mL
2	chipotle chiles en adobo	2
1	bulb roasted garlic	1
8	kaffir lime leaves	8
2 Tbsp.	olive oil	30 mL
1	medium white or red onion, thinly sliced	1
1	red bell pepper, cored and sliced into fine julienne	1
1	yellow bell pepper, cored and sliced into fine julienne	1
2 cups	tender or white corn kernels, fresh or frozen	475 mL
	salt and freshly ground black pepper to taste	
2	limes	2
1/2 cup	chopped fresh cilantro or basil	120 mL
2	ripe avocados, sliced, for garnish (optional)	2

Combine the cumin, garlic and oil. Coat the chicken with the mixture and
refrigerate while preparing the soup. For the best flavour, marinate the chicken
at least 30 minutes before cooking.

Make an infused broth by warming the chicken stock with the chipotles. Do not rinse the chipotles; just include any sauce that clings to the chiles. For a spicier soup, spoon extra sauce into the broth. Squeeze the pulp from the garlic into the stock and add the lime leaves. Heat the stock for about 20 minutes to develop a nice smoky flavour. In the meantime, heat the olive oil in a frying pan and brown the onion lightly. Add the pepper strips and cook until softened. Add the skillet contents to the stock, deglazing the frying pan with a ladleful of stock. Add the corn and season with salt and pepper.

Simmer for about 15 minutes. When you're ready to serve, prepare the chicken. Heat a grill pan or skillet until hot. Sear the chicken on each side until it's brown. Reduce the heat and cook through. Slice the warm chicken into strips.

To serve, divide the chicken among 4 soup bowls. Juice the limes and add it to the soup. Ladle the soup over the chicken and sprinkle with fresh cilantro or basil. If desired, add the sliced avocado to finish.

Puréeing

This is the easy way to purée. Strain the solids from the soup and return the liquid to the cooking pot. Purée the solids with a food mill, blender or food processor, using a bit of the liquid to keep the mixture blending smoothly. Return the purée to the liquid and stir well. This is especially fast and easy when working with large batches.

—Karen Barnaby

Salads

Hearts of Romaine with Asiago Twists

This is a variation on the classic caesar. The bread sticks can be made earlier the same day, but will keep for 3–4 days at room temperature in a tightly covered container. The snake shape of the bread sticks makes for a fun presentation.

Serves 4		Deb Connors
3	cloves garlic, chopped	3
1	egg yolk	1
2 tsp.	Dijon mustard	10 mL
1/4 cup	red wine vinegar	60 mL
1/4 cup	grated Parmesan cheese	60 mL
3/4 cup	extra virgin olive oil	180 mL
1/2 tsp.	freshly ground black pepper	2.5 mL
4	hearts of romaine, washed, dried and coarsely chopped	4
2 Tbsp.	grated Parmesan cheese	30 mL
8	Asiago Twists	8

In a blender combine the garlic, egg yolk, Dijon mustard and red wine vinegar. Add the 1/4 cup (60 mL) Parmesan cheese and blend for 1 minute. Slowly add the olive oil. Season with pepper. If the dressing is too thick you can add a tsp. (5 mL) or so of water.

Place the romaine in a bowl, add the dressing and toss with tongs until the leaves are well coated. Place the salad on 4 plates, sprinkle with the 2 Tbsp. (30 mL) of Parmesan cheese, top with bread sticks and serve.

Squeeze Bottle

Use small squeeze bottles for flavoured oils and dressings, and dessert sauce. They are readily available now in kitchen stores. They help a lot with presentation, making designs on plates, etc.

—Deb Connors

Asiago Twists

If this is more bread sticks than you need, you can divide the dough and freeze the extra for another occasion.

Makes 30 bread sticks

1 tsp.	active dry yeast	5 mL
3 Tbsp.	warm water	45 mL
2 cups	flour	475 mL
1/2 cup	cold water	120 mL
1 1/2 tsp.	vegetable oil	7.5 mL
1 tsp.	salt	5 mL
1/2 cup	grated Asiago cheese	120 mL

Stir the yeast and water together in a small bowl. Let the mixture sit for 5 minutes until the yeast is dissolved.

Place the flour in the bowl of a mixer, then add the dissolved yeast, cold water and oil. Mix with the dough hook at low speed for a few minutes. Increase the mixer speed to medium and beat until the dough comes together, stopping now and again to scrape down the bowl and hook. Add the salt and continue to beat at medium speed for about 10 minutes, until the dough is smooth and elastic. Add the Asiago cheese and beat for 1 minute more. Divide the dough into 2 equal balls. You can refrigerate or freeze the dough at this point.

Line a baking sheet with parchment paper. Using a rolling pin on a lightly floured surface, roll the dough into a rectangle 1/4 inch (.6 cm) thick. Using a pastry cutter or a very sharp knife, cut the dough into 1/4-inch-wide (.6-cm) strips. Place the strips on the lined baking sheet and twist them into S shapes. Allow them to rise, covered, in a warm place for 20–30 minutes.

Preheat the oven to 350°F (175°C). Bake the bread sticks for 12–15 minutes, until golden brown.

Cucumber Salad with Peanuts, Coconut and Lime

This is one of my favourite salads. I can eat it all by itself with a bowl of basmati rice. If you're not feeling that austere, serve it with simple meat dishes or as part of a Thai or Indian feast.

Serves 4		Karen Barnaby
2 Tbsp.	dried unsweetened shredded coconut	30 mL
4 Tbsp.	boiling water	60 mL
1 1/2 cups	English cucumber, diced into 1/4-inch (.6-cm) cubes	360 mL
2	small chilies, finely chopped	2
1/2 cup	freshly roasted peanuts	120 mL
2 Tbsp.	lime juice	30 mL
1/2 tsp.	sugar	2.5 mL
1/2 tsp.	salt	2.5 mL
1 Tbsp.	vegetable oil	15 mL
1/4 tsp.	whole black mustard seeds	1.2 mL

In a small bowl, combine the coconut and boiling water. Let sit until cool. Mix with the cucumber, chilies and peanuts. Mix the lime juice, sugar and salt together. Just before serving, heat the oil over high heat in a small frying pan. Add the mustard seeds. When they pop, add them to the lime juice mixture. Toss with the cucumber mixture and serve immediately.

Travel Essentials

Here is a tip for anyone who goes camping or stays in cabins with "self -contained" kitchens. Bring these items with you every time: a sharp chef's knife, good olive oil, your favourite vinegar, fresh garlic, a pepper grinder, a lemon, a corkscrew and enough salt to boil a pot of pasta.

—Margaret Chisholm

Springtime Open-Face
Asparagus Sandwich (page 6)
and Prawn Spring Rolls with
Lime Cilantro Dipping
Sauce (page 28).

Corn Blini with Smoked Salmon
and Wasabi Cream (page 12)
and Roasted Red Onion and
Shallot Tarts with Thyme
(page 10).

*Butternut Squash and Fava
Bean Soup with Truffle Oil
(page 38).*

Smoke and Lime Chicken Soup
(page 46).

Scallops with Citrus–Vanilla
Bean Vinaigrette (page 66).

Roasted Baby Red Potato Salad with Smoked Salmon (page 68).

Tomatoes Baked Beneath
Spiced Onions (page 74).

Mediterranean Salad
with Tapenade Vinaigrette
(page 53).

Mediterranean Salad with Tapenade Vinaigrette

This salad is best made at the height of summer when the tomatoes, peppers and cucumbers are right out of the garden and not the hothouse.

Serves 8 to 10		Lesley Stowe
2	English cucumbers	2
3	large vine-ripened tomatoes	3
1	each red and yellow bell peppers	1
1	small red onion	1
1/2 cup	prosciutto, diced	120 mL
1/4 cup	capers	60 mL
1 recipe	Tapenade Vinaigrette	1 recipe
1 cup	bocconcini, cut into 1-inch (2.5-cm) cubes	240 mL
2 Tbsp.	chopped mixed fresh herbs	30 mL
	salt and freshly ground black pepper to taste	

Cut the cucumber into quarters lengthwise, then into 1-inch (2.5-cm) pieces. Cut the tomatoes in quarters, then into 1-inch (2.5-cm) chunks. Cut the peppers into 1-inch (2.5-cm) squares. Cut the red onion in half and slice lengthwise with the grain into very fine strips. Toss the vegetables with the prosciutto and capers. Drizzle with vinaigrette and gently stir in the bocconcini and herbs. Season with salt and pepper.

Tapenade Vinaigrette

Makes 3/4 cup (180 mL)		
1/6 cup	sherry vinegar	40 mL
1	clove roasted garlic, mashed	1
1	clove garlic, crushed	1
2 tsp.	black olive paste	10 mL
1/2 cup	extra virgin olive oil	120 mL
	salt and freshly ground black pepper to taste	

Mix together the vinegar, garlic and olive paste. Gradually whisk in the olive oil. Season with salt and pepper.

Bistro Slaw with Caramel Crunch Almonds

This is based on a French bistro classic—salad with endive, pear, blue cheese and hazelnuts. I've interpreted our familiar slaw's creamy dressing and the usual crunch with Gallic choices. Refreshing fennel and Belgian endive are the "cabbage" in this recipe, while apples and pears give it authenticity. Shopping in my neighbourhood, I discovered toasted sugary almonds from France. Et voilà!

Serves 8 for lunch or 12 as a side dish		Glenys Morgan
2	lemons	2
2 tsp.	Dijon mustard	10 mL
2 Tbsp.	honey	30 mL
	salt and freshly ground black pepper to taste	
1/2 cup	canola or mild olive oil	120 mL
3 oz.	blue cheese, such as mild Danish, Gorgonzola or Roquefort	85 g
2	fennel bulbs, trimmed of stalks	2
2	Granny Smith apples, or any apple with a crisp texture	2
2	ripe pears in season, such as Bosc or Bartlett	2
3	Belgian endive	3
1/2 cup	sugar-coated caramel almonds, coarsely chopped	120 mL

It's important to have the dressing prepared before slicing the crunchy parts of the slaw, so you can toss the vegetables in the dressing immediately to prevent browning. Juice the lemons and whisk together with the Dijon mustard. This activates the starch in the mustard and creates a creamier dressing. Add the honey, season lightly with salt and pepper and add the oil, whisking until creamy. Taste for sweetness and adjust to your tastebuds. At this point all the cheese may be whisked into the dressing for a very creamy consistency, or you can whisk a portion into the dressing and reserve some to sprinkle on the salad at the end.

Remove any soft, slightly brown layers from the outside of the fennel bulb. Like a cabbage, the layers underneath should be crisp. Cut away the core and shave the fennel into fine strips. Toss with the dressing to coat.

Leave the apples and pears unpeeled for colour. Halve them and core with a melon scoop for a nice look, then thinly slice them. Add them to the dressing and toss to coat. Quarter the Belgian endive and slice away the core. Cut it in thin strips lengthwise and add it to the salad. Toss again.

The slaw is ready to serve and since all the components are naturally tender, it doesn't need to age before serving. Just before serving, sprinkle the crunchy chopped almonds over the salad.

Minted Feta Salad

I love the flavour of mint in savoury foods. Use a high-quality extra virgin olive oil, preferably one that is cold pressed. This simple salad is perfect served alongside Pomegranate Roast Lamb (page 114).

Serves 4		Margaret Chisholm
5 oz.	feta cheese, preferably goat cheese	140 g
1 cup	mint leaves	240 mL
5 cups	romaine lettuce leaves, cut into 2-inch (5-cm) pieces	1.2 L
4 Tbsp.	extra virgin olive oil	60 mL
1/4 tsp.	sea salt	1.2 mL
1/2 tsp.	freshly ground black pepper	2.5 mL
2 Tbsp.	freshly squeezed lemon juice	30 mL

Crumble the goat cheese. Tear the mint leaves into pieces and combine with the romaine in a salad bowl. Drizzle with the olive oil and toss well to coat evenly. Add the salt, pepper and lemon juice and toss well. Sprinkle with the feta and toss again gently. Serve immediately.

Roasted Beets with Tarragon Vinaigrette

*I hated beets as a child but now I love them, especially roasted.
Roasting gives them a wonderful caramelized flavour. This dish can be
a side dish or salad. In cooler weather I like to serve the roasted beets
tossed in the vinaigrette while still warm. In summer roast golden beets,
slice them thinly, toss them in the vinaigrette and serve them cold.*

Serves 4		Mary Mackay
8	medium beets, tops trimmed to 1/2 inch (1.2 cm)	8
1/2 tsp.	Dijon mustard	2.5 mL
1/2 tsp.	finely chopped shallot	2.5 mL
1/4 tsp.	sea salt	1.2 mL
1/4 tsp.	sugar	1.2 mL
2 Tbsp.	raspberry vinegar	30 mL
3 Tbsp.	olive oil	45 mL
2 tsp.	chopped fresh tarragon	10 mL
	freshly cracked black pepper to taste	

Preheat the oven to 450°F (230°C). Scrub the beets under water and pat
them dry with paper towel. Place them in a small roasting pan and roast for
15 minutes. Reduce the heat to 350°F (175°C) and roast until tender, about
another 60–80 minutes.

In a small bowl whisk together the Dijon mustard, shallot, salt, sugar and
raspberry vinegar. Slowly whisk in the olive oil. Stir in the tarragon and
black pepper.

Slice the warm roasted beets in half. Toss them in the tarragon vinaigrette
and let sit 5 minutes. The beets can be served warm or cold.

Basics

Buy a good chef's knife and keep it
sharp. Throw out your ground black
pepper. Buy good sea salt and
high-quality extra virgin olive oil.

—Margaret Chisholm

Middle Eastern Couscous Salad

Middle Eastern couscous is not the common small-grained couscous most of us are familiar with. This is a larger toasted variety that swells to the size of tiny peas. The texture is far more interesting than regular couscous. Pair it with Pomegranate Roast Lamb (page 114). Leftover salad is particularly good for lunch the next day.

Serves 6 to 8		*Caren McSherry-Valagao*
1/2 cup	sweet port or Madeira	120 mL
1 cup	Black Mission figs, cut into quarters	240 mL
3 Tbsp.	unsalted butter	45 mL
1	large Spanish onion, sliced	1
2	cloves garlic, minced	2
1/2	jalapeño pepper, finely diced (optional)	1/2
1 tsp.	ground cinnamon	5 mL
1 tsp.	saffron threads, pounded into a powder	5 mL
1 1/2 tsp.	ground cumin	7.5 mL
1 tsp.	ground cardamom	5 mL
5 cups	chicken stock	1.2 L
3 cups	toasted Middle Eastern couscous	720 mL
2	large red bell peppers, roasted and diced	2
1/2 cup	each chopped fresh parsley and cilantro	120 mL
1/4 cup	chopped fresh mint	60 mL
	sea salt and freshly ground black pepper to taste	
1 cup	natural pistachio nuts, toasted and chopped	240 mL

Heat the port or Madeira in a small pot, add the figs and simmer for about 5 minutes, or until most of the port is absorbed. Set aside.

Melt the butter in a large frying pan, and add the onion, garlic and jalapeño. Sauté until the onion is golden brown. Add the cinnamon, saffron, cumin and cardamom, and continue to cook for another minute. Bring the chicken stock to a boil, add the couscous and let it simmer for about 5 minutes, or until most of the stock is absorbed. Stir in the onion spice mixture, diced peppers, marinated figs and port. Fold in the fresh herbs, and adjust the seasoning with salt and pepper. Turn onto a decorative serving platter and garnish with the toasted pistachios.

Thai Salad Niçoise

An irreverent take on a classic but no one seems to mind when the dressing is fat-free and there's salmon on the plate. Prawns are also a choice. The bright citrus dressing really stands out when made with the trio of herbs. Use it as a marinade for chicken or single out an item from the salad and dress it up for dinner.

Serves 6		Glenys Morgan
24	green beans, stemmed and trimmed	24
12–16	asparagus spears, trimmed	12–16
1 lb.	nugget potatoes, or larger potatoes quartered	454 g
4–6	ripe tomatoes, quartered	4–6
1/2	English cucumber, thinly sliced	1/2
1	red onion, halved and sliced into julienne	1
1–2	red bell peppers, cored and cut into julienne	1–2
1 1/2 lbs.	salmon fillets, skin removed, cut into pieces	680 g
2 Tbsp.	olive oil	30 mL
	sea salt and freshly ground black pepper to taste	
6	cloves garlic, finely minced	6
1/4 cup	brown sugar	60 mL
2	limes, zest and juice	2
1/4 cup	nam pla (Thai fish sauce)	60 mL
1 Tbsp.	sambal oelek (Thai hot sauce)	15 mL
1 cup	chopped cilantro, mint, basil or a combination	240 mL

Outfit a large saucepan with a steaming basket, preferably a bamboo steamer. Steam the beans and asparagus over rapidly boiling water until crisp-tender, then refresh in a bowl of ice water to preserve their colour. Steam the potatoes until fork tender, replenishing the water if necessary.

Have all the cooked and fresh vegetables prepared and ready for arranging and dressing. Except for the tomato, they can be prepared ahead and stored in the refrigerator until needed.

Rub the salmon fillets with half the olive oil and season lightly with salt and pepper. Heat the remaining oil in a non-stick skillet. Sear the fillets skin side up. When nicely browned, turn them and reduce the heat to slowly cook them through. The salmon should be firm to the touch when cooked. (You can also grill or steam the salmon if you prefer.)

Arrange the vegetables on a large platter or individual plates. Top with the salmon fillets. Whisk together the garlic, sugar, lime juice and zest, nam pla, sambal oelek and herbs. The dressing may be made ahead but the herbs must be added just before serving to avoid darkening. Spoon the fresh dressing over the platter or pass it in small bowls to each diner.

Grilled Asparagus with Grapefruit Vinaigrette

Not everything improves with grilling, but asparagus definitely lends itself to this style of cooking. Be careful not to overchar it as that flavour can become too prominent. If you don't have access to a grill, try roasting the asparagus in the oven—the flavour will be quite different but it is still very good. When asparagus is not in season, replace it with haricots vert, the skinny French green bean.

Serves 8		Lesley Stowe
2 lbs.	jumbo asparagus spears	900 g
2 Tbsp.	extra virgin olive oil	30 mL
	salt and freshly ground black pepper to taste	
2	pink grapefruit, segments separated and membranes removed	2
1 recipe	Grapefruit Vinaigrette (page 60)	1 recipe
2 oz.	Asiago cheese	57 g
1/3 cup	toasted pine nuts	80 mL
2 Tbsp.	chopped chives	30 mL
	freshly ground black pepper to taste	

Heat a barbecue or broiler to medium-hot.

Toss the asparagus with the olive oil, salt and pepper. Grill or broil until charred or slightly blackened, about 4 minutes. Let cool.

Arrange the asparagus spears on a plate and place the grapefruit segments across the middle of the asparagus. Drizzle with the vinaigrette. Using a vegetable peeler, shave the cheese into thin shavings. Garnish with pine nuts, Asiago, chives and pepper. Serve extra dressing on the side.

Grapefruit Vinaigrette

Makes 3/4 cup (180 mL)

1 Tbsp.	pink grapefruit juice	15 mL
2	pink grapefruit segments, peeled	2
1 tsp.	finely chopped fresh ginger	5 mL
1 tsp.	finely chopped shallots	5 mL
	juice of half a lime	
1/4 cup	extra virgin olive oil	60 mL
	salt and freshly ground black pepper to taste	

Purée the grapefruit juice, grapefruit segments, ginger, shallots and lime juice in a blender. With the motor running, add the olive oil in a steady stream until it is all incorporated. Season with salt and pepper.

Presentation

A tailor can update a suit and a cook can update a dish just by giving it a new shape. Stylish versions of comfort food favourites appear on the most popular menus—it's just the look that's new. Cut a brownie into elongated wedges instead of the classic square. Bake your favourite scalloped potato recipe in individual ramekins for each plate—they can even be unmolded for an elegant presentation. Tie perfectly cooked asparagus into bundles with ribbons of leek or green onion, pretty on the plate and easy to pick up at the buffet table. Cut a simple cake into squares and ice each one to create individual cakes. Take your best cookie recipe and make bite-size cookies by cutting down the baking time and the size. Or better yet, present tiny portions of your three favourite desserts on a large plate. The comfort is in using a tried and true recipe, the rest is style.

—Glenys Morgan

Cilantro Pesto Penne Salad

*I adore the flavour of cilantro, but this was not always so. My sister
and I travelled to South America long before cilantro was a fixture on
our local grocery shelves. It was in everything. We hated it. We thought
it tasted like detergent. Somehow, as with most people who persevere
with this herb, we learned to like it. This pesto can be used in the same
ways as the more familiar basil pesto and it keeps its great, bright green
colour. I was looking for a way to update pasta salad when I created
this recipe. Serve it with Grilled Prawns with Smoked Pepper
Tartar Sauce (page 128).*

Serves 6 to 8		Margaret Chisholm
1 Tbsp.	coarse salt	15 mL
1 lb.	penne pasta	454 g
2 cups	cilantro leaves	480 mL
1 1/2 cups	fresh spinach	360 mL
1	clove garlic, chopped	1
3 Tbsp.	olive oil	45 mL
2 Tbsp.	lime juice	30 mL
3/4 cup	Parmesan cheese	160 mL
1	red bell pepper, sliced into thin strips	1
1 cup	cherry tomatoes, halved	240 mL
1 cup	snow peas, cut into 1-inch (2.5-cm) pieces	240 mL
4 oz.	Asiago cheese, grated	113 g

Bring a large pot of water to a boil over high heat and add the coarse salt.
Add the pasta and boil until it's al dente. Drain and rinse with cold water.
Set aside.

Combine the cilantro, spinach, garlic, olive oil and lime juice in a food
processor. Process until a smooth paste forms, scraping down the sides of the
bowl occasionally. Place the mixture in a large bowl and stir in the Parmesan
cheese. Add the pasta and toss well to coat it evenly. Add the red pepper,
cherry tomatoes, snow peas and Asiago cheese. Toss and serve.

Soba Noodle and Duck Salad

Soba is a Japanese noodle that contains buckwheat flour, giving the noodle a brownish hue. I use barbecued duck from a good Chinese take-out—they have had lots of practice cooking it perfectly and you don't have to clean a greasy pan. A perfect summer companion either at home or on the beach, this updated version of the traditional pasta salad will become a seasonal favourite.

Serves 6 to 8		Caren McSherry-Valagao
1	barbecued duck	1
1	8-oz. (227-g) package soba noodles	1
1	large shallot, finely minced	1
4 Tbsp.	soy sauce	60 mL
2 Tbsp.	rice vinegar	30 mL
1 Tbsp.	chopped fermented black beans	15 mL
1 Tbsp.	minced fresh ginger	15 mL
2 Tbsp.	sesame oil, preferably Kadoya brand	30 mL
2	cloves garlic, minced	2
1 Tbsp.	chili paste (optional)	15 mL
3/4 cup	roasted grapeseed oil	180 mL
1	red pepper, julienned	1
1	large carrot, julienned	1
1	zucchini, pulp and seeds removed and green portion julienned	1
1 cup	chopped fresh cilantro	240 mL
2 Tbsp.	chopped fresh mint	30 mL
2 Tbsp.	black sesame seeds, toasted	30 mL
2 Tbsp.	white sesame seeds, toasted	30 mL
	chive blossoms (optional)	

Remove the meat from the duck, discarding the skin and bones. Shred the meat and set aside. Cook the soba noodles to al dente, rinse in cold water, drain well and set aside.

Prepare the dressing by whisking together the shallot, soy sauce, rice vinegar, black beans, ginger, sesame oil, garlic and chili paste. Slowly pour the oil into the bowl, whisking the entire time. Taste for seasoning. Pour the dressing over the drained soba noodles, add all the julienned vegetables, the cilantro, mint and shredded duck. Toss well to coat evenly.

Turn the noodle salad onto a serving platter, sprinkle with sesame seeds and garnish with chive blossoms if available.

· · · · · ·

Quick Fix:

Fast-Choppy-Chop Salad

This was called "you know, the usual thing with brown rice" until choppy-chop was coined. It is very satisfying.

Wash and cook 2 measuring units of brown basmati rice with a bit more water than used for white rice. Then chop 2–3 tomatoes, and a piece of English cucumber into small dice. Chopping the vegetables in tiny dice will give a better taste and texture to the salad, as you get a mouthful of different tastes all at once. Thinly slice a wedge of red or green cabbage, coarsely chop a small handful of cilantro and/or parsley, mint or whatever kind of herbs you have on hand, thinly slice some green onion or white onion and dice avocado. Sprouted bean mix, daikon sprouts, cooked green beans or asparagus often find their way into my bowl.

For the dressing, drain the juice from a large can of solid white tuna or sockeye salmon into a bowl and add a lot of lemon or lime juice and a lot of salt to it. Remember that it has to cover a lot of unseasoned rice and juicy vegetables. All of this sits until the rice is cooked. When the rice is done I toss the vegetables with the dressing and check for seasoning. I may add some *gomasio* (a blend of salt and ground, toasted sesame seeds) and always a generous shake of ground morita chilies. The rice goes into bowls and is covered by the vegetables. The canned fish is crumbled and goes on top.

You can vary this in many ways. Adding Dijon mustard to the dressing and using cooked green beans, pitted black olives, capers, basil and canned tuna will give you a niçoise-style Choppy-Chop.

—Karen Barnaby

Another Bread Salad . . .

This salad comes with its own edible salad bowl, a hollowed-out round loaf of bread. My favourite part of bread making is shaping round loaves—for a baker, there is nothing quite like the feel of cupping a piece of dough in your hands. At our bakery the majority of the loaves sold are oblong in shape. I think people pass up the round loaves because they are not the right shape for making sandwiches. I am always looking for ways to get people to use the round loaves so I can continue to shape them. This recipe combines toasted cheesy croutons with roasted artichokes, red onions, red peppers, black olives and fresh thyme. When the salad is finished the bread salad bowl can be torn up and enjoyed with the rest of your meal.

Serves 4 to 6		Mary Mackay
1	14-oz. (398-mL) can artichoke hearts, drained and cut into quarters	1
1	small red onion, thinly sliced	1
1 tsp.	olive oil	5 mL
1/4 tsp.	sea salt	1.2 mL
1	1-lb. (454-g) round loaf of bread, preferably sourdough	1
1/4 cup	crumbled goat cheese (chèvre)	60 mL
1/4 cup	grated Parmesan cheese	60 mL
1/4 tsp.	Dijon mustard	1.2 mL
1/4 tsp.	sea salt	1.2 mL
2 Tbsp.	white wine vinegar	30 mL
1/4 cup	olive oil	60 mL
1 tsp.	chopped fresh thyme	5 mL
1/2 cup	sliced roasted red pepper	120 mL
16	kalamata olives, pitted and cut in half	16
	freshly cracked black pepper to taste	
4	sprigs fresh thyme	4

Preheat the oven to 400°F (200°C). Toss the artichoke hearts and red onion in the 1 tsp. (5 mL) olive oil and 1/4 tsp. (1.2 mL) salt. Spread out on a baking sheet, avoiding the outer edges of the pan. Bake for 15 minutes. Toss the vegetables and bake for another 13 minutes. The vegetables will be lightly browned. Set the artichokes and onions aside to cool.

Using a serrated knife, slice off the top of the round loaf, a quarter of the way down. Save the top as a lid for the bread salad bowl. Use your fingers to gently pull out the interior of the loaf. Work your way around the inside edges, being careful not to make holes in the crust. Set the bread salad bowl aside. Tear the bread into bite-size pieces. Place them on a baking sheet and sprinkle with the goat cheese and Parmesan cheese. Bake for 8 minutes. Set the croutons aside to cool.

In a bowl whisk together the Dijon mustard, the remaining 1/4 tsp. (1.2 mL) salt and white wine vinegar. Whisk in the 1/4 cup (60 mL) olive oil and the chopped thyme.

Toss the artichokes, red onions, red pepper and kalamata olives in the thyme vinaigrette. Stir in the cheese croutons. Season with pepper. Transfer the salad to the bread salad bowl and garnish with fresh thyme sprigs. To serve, place the bread salad bowl on a cutting board with the bread lid resting on the side of the bowl.

Pitting Olives

Use the bottom of a small heavy saucepan or sauté pan to press the pits out of olives.

—Lesley Stowe

Scallops with Citrus–Vanilla Bean Vinaigrette

This light summer salad is quick and easy to make. The citrus–vanilla bean is a lovely and unusual combination. If you are unable to locate vanilla bean, you can leave it out or substitute a small amount of fresh thyme or chives after the vinaigrette comes out of the blender.

Serves 4		Deb Connors
1 cup	fresh orange juice	240 mL
2 tsp.	honey	10 mL
1/2	vanilla bean	1/2
2 Tbsp.	rice wine vinegar	30 mL
1/2 cup	canola oil	120 mL
	salt and freshly ground black pepper to taste	
2	small heads of butter lettuce	2
1 Tbsp.	olive oil	15 mL
12	large scallops	12
	salt and freshly ground black pepper to taste	
2	oranges, peeled and cut into segments	2
8	strawberries, hulled and sliced	8
8	small edible blossoms	8

To make the vinaigrette, place the orange juice and honey in a small saucepan over high heat. Bring to a boil and reduce the heat to simmer. Using a small sharp knife and a cutting board, cut the vanilla bean in half lengthwise. Holding the vanilla bean over the pot, use the knife to loosen some of the little black seeds from the bean into the orange juice. Place the pod in the juice and continue to simmer until the juice reduces to a glaze, about 1/4 cup (60 mL).

When the juice is cool, remove the vanilla pod with your fingers, squeezing it to loosen more seeds. Using a small rubber spatula, scrape the contents of the saucepan into a blender. With the motor running, add the rice wine vinegar, then slowly add the canola oil. Season with salt and pepper and set aside.

Wash the butter lettuce and separate it into leaves. Pat it dry and refrigerate.

Heat the olive oil in a small pan. Season the scallops with salt and pepper. When the oil is hot, sauté the scallops over high heat for 1 minute per side, until they are nicely coloured on the outside. Do not overcook.

Arrange the butter lettuce on 4 small plates. Arrange the oranges and strawberries over the lettuce. Place 3 warm scallops on each salad and drizzle with the vinaigrette. Garnish with edible blossoms.

Potato Salad with Tuna, Caper and Anchovy Vinaigrette

This salad is a meal in itself. Serve with roasted red peppers that have been splashed with a bit of balsamic vinegar, sliced ripe tomatoes and grilled bread.

Serves 4 to 6		Karen Barnaby
1 1/2 lbs.	evenly sized small red potatoes	680 g
2 Tbsp.	lemon juice	30 mL
1/4 tsp.	salt	1.2 mL
2 Tbsp.	small drained capers	30 mL
4 Tbsp.	olive oil	60 mL
2 Tbsp.	lemon juice	30 mL
1	clove garlic, minced	1
1	7-oz. (198-g) can oil-packed light tuna	1
6	oil-packed anchovy fillets, finely chopped	6
2 Tbsp.	finely diced onion	30 mL
4 Tbsp.	finely chopped parsley	60 mL

In a large pot, cover the potatoes with ample water and bring to a boil. Cook until the potatoes are just tender when pierced with the tip of a small knife, 15–20 minutes. Drain. When cool enough to handle, cut into 1-inch (2.5-cm) pieces. Combine with 2 Tbsp. (30 mL) lemon juice and the salt. Toss well and let cool.

Finely chop half of the capers. Combine the olive oil, remaining 2 Tbsp. (30 mL) lemon juice and garlic. Add the tuna with the oil, anchovies, chopped and whole capers, onion and parsley. Stir well, crumbling the tuna lightly. Add to the potatoes and toss well. Cover and refrigerate until serving.

Roasted Baby Red Potato Salad with Smoked Salmon

This salad is best served soon after it is mixed with the dressing so that the roasted skins stay a little crispy. The smoked salmon makes it deluxe. If you don't have smoked salmon, add 1/2 cup (120 mL) freshly grated Parmesan cheese instead. If you plan to take it on a picnic, which you should, bring the dressing separately in a little jar and toss the potatoes with the dressing just before serving.

Serves 4		Margaret Chisholm
1 1/4 lbs.	baby red potatoes, quartered	565 g
1 Tbsp.	olive oil	15 mL
1/4 tsp.	salt	1.2 mL
3/4 lb.	green beans, cut into 2-inch (5-cm) pieces	340 g
1/2	small red onion, thinly sliced	1/2
1/4 cup	sliced chives or green onion	60 mL
3 1/2 oz.	smoked salmon, sliced in strips	100 g
1 1/2 Tbsp.	red wine vinegar	22.5 mL
1 1/2 Tbsp.	Dijon mustard	22.5 mL
1/4 tsp.	salt	1.2 mL
1/2 tsp.	freshly ground black pepper	2.5 mL
5 Tbsp.	olive oil	75 mL

Preheat the oven to 375°F (190°C). Toss the potatoes in the 1 Tbsp. (15 mL) olive oil and season with the salt. Spread the potatoes on a baking sheet and bake for approximately 30 minutes, or until soft. Set aside to cool. Blanch the green beans in boiling water for 1 minute, drain and plunge into ice water to stop the cooking and fix the colour. Drain well.

Combine the potatoes, green beans, red onion, chives or green onion and smoked salmon in a bowl.

Whisk together the red wine vinegar, Dijon mustard, salt and pepper in a small bowl. Slowly drizzle in the 5 Tbsp. (75 mL) olive oil while continuing to whisk. Just before serving, toss the salad with the dressing.

Warm Red Cabbage Salad with Pancetta and Hazelnuts

Cabbage is a vegetable that is underused and overabused. Too many people have bad memories of limp boiled cabbage from their youth. I am hoping you will change your mind about cabbage with this recipe.

Serves 8		Lesley Stowe
1 lb.	red cabbage	454 g
1/4 lb.	best-quality thinly sliced pancetta	113 g
1/2 cup	fruity extra virgin olive oil	120 mL
1 tsp.	minced garlic	5 mL
1 tsp.	honey	5 mL
1/3 cup	red wine vinegar	80 mL
1/2 tsp.	each sea salt and black pepper	2.5 mL
8	sprigs watercress, for garnish	8
4 oz.	goat cheese	113 g
1/2 cup	toasted hazelnuts, roughly chopped	120 mL

Core and finely shred the cabbage; set aside. Heat a large frying pan over medium-low heat. Add the pancetta and cook until it is slightly browned and crisp. Cook in batches if necessary. Drain, chop roughly and set aside. Combine the olive oil with the garlic, honey, vinegar, salt and pepper. Taste and correct the seasoning.

In a large sauté pan over moderate-high heat, briefly warm the dressing. Add the cabbage and toss quickly for 2–3 minutes, just to wilt it slightly. Add the chopped pancetta. Divide the salad among 8 warm salad plates and garnish with watercress, crumbled goat cheese and toasted hazelnuts.

Skinning Hazelnuts

To skin larger amounts of toasted hazelnuts, place the hazelnuts, still warm from the oven, in a small cotton drawstring bag, tie the top very tightly, and place the bag, by itself, in the dryer on a low setting for about 10 minutes. This will rub the skins off the hazelnuts most efficiently. The most important step is the tying of the bag!

—Deb Connors

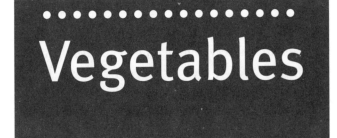

Vegetables

Grilled Asparagus with Sesame Drizzle

There is no bad asparagus, just delicious thick, thin and in between. The thick spears are buttery and the thin ones have the green taste of spring. My preferred way to cook them is dry grilling. The method is a bit odd but I stand by the flavour. For a buffet or elegant first course, serve side by side with Grilled Asparagus with Grapefruit Vinaigrette, page 59.

Serves 4 to 6		Glenys Morgan
3 Tbsp.	sesame seeds	45 mL
2 Tbsp.	sugar	30 mL
3 Tbsp.	soy sauce, preferably Japanese	45 mL
1 Tbsp.	mirin or rice wine vinegar	15 mL
1 lb.	asparagus, washed and coarse ends trimmed	454 g
1/2 tsp.	sea salt, preferably coarse	2.5 mL
	freshly ground black pepper to taste	
1 Tbsp.	olive oil	15 mL

In a small skillet over medium-high heat, toast the sesame seeds, shaking the pan, until the seeds are toasted light brown. Crush the seeds in a mortar and pestle. (If you do not have a mortar and pestle, blend them in a blender on high.) When the sesame seeds are finely crushed add half the sugar, the soy sauce and mirin. Taste for sweetness. Add the remaining sugar to taste. The sauce should be sweet and tangy.

Choose a large heavy skillet or griddle; cast iron is ideal and non-stick will be damaged by the heat. Heat the pan over high heat until it's searing hot. Lower the heat and immediately add the asparagus in a single layer, preferably pointing in the same direction. Cook in batches if necessary, reheating the pan to searing hot between each batch. As the asparagus brightens in colour and gets little charred spots, rotate the spears to cook them on all sides. The cooked asparagus will be bright green and moist looking from its moisture steaming out. Season with salt and pepper and drizzle with olive oil.

Arrange the asparagus on a platter and spoon the sesame drizzle over the spears. Serve warm or at room temperature, as a salad or side dish.

Grilled Endive

You can make this great side dish on the grill or the stove top. It works equally well at an elegant dinner party or a backyard supper. Do not marinate the endive for too long as it will darken.

Serves 4		Deb Connors
4 Tbsp.	extra virgin olive oil	60 mL
2 Tbsp.	good-quality balsamic vinegar	30 mL
1/2	lemon, juice only	1/2
1/2 tsp.	sea salt	2.5 mL
1/2 tsp.	freshly ground black pepper	2.5 mL
4	Belgian endive, cut in half	4

In a small bowl combine the olive oil, balsamic vinegar, lemon juice, salt and pepper. Add the endive and toss to coat. Marinate for 20–30 minutes. Grill the endive for 2 minutes per side over medium heat, until it is well marked, or in a sauté pan over medium heat until the cut side is browned.

Condiment Tricks

Condiment junkies admit our fridges are full of jars that we never finish. Those last spoonfuls, blended with unsalted butter, create tasty compound butters that will breathe life into a simple dish. Apricot jam, peach chutney and a bit of mint jelly make a great butter for a salmon fillet. Combine herbs from the garden, roasted garlic, a few sun-dried tomatoes and even regular salsa from the corner store. Mix the last of a tomato salsa with bits of pesto. Blend in enough softened butter to make a smooth consistency, roll it into a log in plastic wrap and freeze. Slice rounds onto the top of warm pasta, grilled chicken, baked potato or corn on the cob, or use it to baste prawns on the grill. As an alternative to butter, purée it with your favourite oil and freeze it in ice-cube trays.

—Glenys Morgan

Tomatoes Baked Beneath Spiced Onions

These spicy tomatoes can be served with any plainly cooked meat, fish or fowl. I especially like them with steamed spinach. Garnish with a bit of yogurt or sour cream for a luxurious finish.

Serves 4 to 6		Karen Barnaby
2 lbs.	ripe tomatoes, cut in half crosswise	900 g
1 1/2 tsp.	salt	7.5 mL
1 1/2 tsp.	ground cumin	7.5 mL
1 Tbsp.	ground coriander	15 mL
1 tsp.	coarsely ground black pepper	5 mL
1/4 tsp.	turmeric	1.2 mL
1/4 tsp.	cayenne pepper	1.2 mL
2 Tbsp.	vegetable oil	30 mL
2	medium onions, cut in half crosswise and cut into 1/4-inch (.6-cm) slices	2
2	cloves garlic, minced	2
2 tsp.	minced fresh ginger	10 mL

Preheat the oven to 350ºF (175ºC). With a small spoon, remove the seeds from the tomato halves. Place the tomato halves cut side up in a baking dish that will hold them snugly in a single layer without overlapping. Bake uncovered for 1/2 hour.

While the tomatoes are baking, combine the salt, cumin, coriander, pepper, turmeric and cayenne. Heat the oil in a large frying pan over medium heat. Add the onion, garlic and ginger. Cook over low heat, stirring frequently, until the onions are very soft and translucent. Add the spice mix and cook for a few moments longer.

Remove the tomatoes from the oven and spread the onion mixture evenly over them. Return to the oven and bake for 45 minutes longer. Let sit for 10 minutes before serving.

Roasted Carrots with Saffron Chili Oil

Fresh ingredients available at the market often influence me to put recipes together, and sometimes I want to create recipes for my growing collection of glassware. One of my favourites is a clear glass jar with a red chili pepper for its top. This recipe makes more saffron chili oil than required, so I can fill my pepper jar and enjoy the infused oil brushed on grilled vegetables or spread on good crusty bread. Try it on fish, chicken, or a tomato and bocconcini salad. Saffron chili oil can be kept in the fridge for a couple of weeks.

Serves 4 to 6		Mary Mackay
1/2 tsp.	saffron threads	2.5 mL
1 Tbsp.	warm water	15 mL
1/4 cup	canola oil	60 mL
1 1/2 tsp.	finely chopped shallot	7.5 mL
1/2 tsp.	dried red pepper flakes	2.5 mL
1/4 tsp.	sea salt	1.2 mL
1/4 tsp.	finely chopped orange zest (zest of 1 orange)	1.2 mL
16	small carrots, green tops trimmed to 1/2 inch (1.2 cm)	16

Crush the saffron threads in a mortar and pestle or a spice grinder. Stir the crushed saffron and water together in a small dish, and set aside while you prepare the oil.

Bring the canola oil, shallot and red pepper flakes to a simmer in a small pan over medium heat. Reduce the heat to low and cook for another 2 minutes. Stir in the sea salt and let the oil cool.

Stir the saffron and orange zest into the cooled oil. Place the saffron chili oil in the fridge until you're ready to use it. Stir or shake before using.

Preheat the oven to 450°F (230°C). Scrub the carrots under water and pat them dry. Toss the carrots in a bowl with 1 tsp. (5 mL) of the saffron chili oil. Place the carrots in a single layer on a baking sheet. Roast for 15 minutes, then turn them over and roast another 10–15 minutes, until browned.

To serve, pile the carrots on a platter and drizzle with saffron chili oil. Serve with extra saffron chili oil for dipping.

Roasted Corn and Zucchini with Truffle Oil

This recipe is a perfect example of how to develop big flavours by charring and roasting vegetables. Serve it as is, or with polenta or over pasta. The truffle oil is available in specialty food stores. It is entirely optional, so don't let it put you off.

Serves 4		Karen Barnaby
1 lb.	ripe plum tomatoes	454 g
2	large red bell peppers	2
1	dried red chili pepper, crushed (or to taste)	1
3 Tbsp.	olive oil	45 mL
1/2 cup	finely chopped onion	120 mL
3	cloves garlic, minced	3
	salt to taste	
2 cups	corn kernels, fresh or frozen	475 mL
2	medium zucchini	2
2 tsp.	truffle oil	10 mL
12	fresh basil leaves	12

Preheat the broiler, adjusting the oven rack to approximately 6 inches (15 cm) below the heat source. Place the tomatoes and peppers on a baking sheet. Broil, turning to blacken the skins on all sides. Remove from the broiler and let cool.

Keeping the blackened skins on the peppers and tomatoes, cut them in half and remove the seeds. Place in a sieve to drain for half an hour. Using a food processor or blender, purée the peppers, tomatoes and chili pepper until smooth. The mixture will be quite thick.

In a medium-sized pot, heat the olive oil over medium heat. Add the onion and garlic and sauté until the onion is translucent. Add the tomato and pepper mixture and simmer over low heat for 15–20 minutes. Season with salt. The mixture may be prepared up to a day in advance.

Preheat the oven to 400°F (200°C). Spread the corn kernels in a single layer on a baking sheet and bake for 15–20 minutes, stirring occasionally, until the corn is flecked with brown spots. Add to the sauce.

Trim the zucchini and cut it into 1/4-inch (.6-cm) lengthwise slices. Place it on a baking sheet and brush lightly with olive oil. Turn the broiler to high and broil the zucchini on the uppermost shelf until browned on both sides. Cut into 1-inch (2.5-cm) pieces.

Reheat the sauce and simmer for 5 minutes, adding a bit of water if it seems too thick. Add the zucchini, truffle oil and fresh basil and heat through.

• • • • • •
Quick Fix:

Corn with Guacamole

If you like corn chips with guacamole, you can bring the whole idea closer to its roots and have corn with guacamole. I love slathering the cool guacamole on the hot corn, studying the green swipe flecked with red on the gold background, and then chowing down on the crunchy cob.

I am a fanatic about making guacamole. Lime juice, not lemon, must be used, no food processor is used to blend it, and no garlic, cumin or shocking seasonings should distract your tongue from its smooth, creamy greenness. Since I'm on a band-wagon, I'll take the opportunity to moan over the omnipresent presence of Peaches and Cream corn. Where has all the good, yellow, corny-flavoured corn gone?

To make guacamole, peel and pit 3 ripe Haas avocados. Place them in a bowl and coarsely mash them with a fork. Chunks of avocado are just fine— it shouldn't be completely smooth. Stir in 3/8 tsp. (2 mL) salt and 2 Tbsp. (30 mL) lime juice. Stir in a seeded and finely diced tomato, 1 Tbsp. (15 mL) coarsely chopped cilantro, 2 Tbsp. (30 mL) finely chopped white onion and a finely chopped fresh hot chili pepper. Add pepper to taste. Cover and refrigerate. Serve it within half an hour.

—Karen Barnaby

Baby Artichokes au Gratin

Grilled, boiled, hot, cold, marinated or even tinned, artichokes are fast becoming the veggie of choice. I am very fond of the baby ones, for one easy reason—they have no choke or thistle. All you do is peel back the green leaves and trim the base. Try this recipe, for an easy, unintimidating preparation of California's thorny export. Serve it with Cornish Game Hens Stuffed with Olives and Thyme (page 100).

Serves 6		Caren McSherry-Valagao
18	fresh baby artichokes	18
2 Tbsp.	white vinegar or lemon juice	30 mL
3 Tbsp.	good-quality olive oil	45 mL
4	shallots, peeled and minced	4
3	cloves garlic, minced	3
1/2 cup	minced fresh parsley	120 mL
1/3 cup	white wine	80 mL
	sea salt and freshly ground black pepper to taste	
1/3 cup	grated Pecorino Romano cheese	80 mL
1/3 cup	grated Parmesan cheese	80 mL

Bend all the leaves to remove them from the artichokes and carefully pare the stem. As you work, place the cleaned artichokes into a large bowl of water with the white vinegar or lemon juice to prevent discoloration. Boil the chokes for 10–15 minutes, drain, and refresh under cold water. For a more interesting look to the final dish, cut 6 of the artichokes in half and leave the rest whole.

Heat the oil in a shallow skillet or sauté pan and add the shallots and garlic. Sauté for a few minutes, then toss in the artichokes, parsley and wine. Adjust the seasoning with salt and pepper. Simmer until the artichokes are cooked through, about 5 minutes.

Transfer the mixture to a gratin dish, sprinkle with the cheeses and broil until the cheese begins to bubble and brown. Serve with a crusty bread.

Honey and Thyme Roasted Winter Vegetables

This recipe calls for a combination of vegetables (who knew parsnips could taste so good?), but you could do any one vegetable this way on its own. Fennel in particular is superb. Spread the vegetables out loosely on the roasting pan to make sure they are well roasted. This will pair well with any of our lamb dishes.

Serves 6		Margaret Chisholm
3 Tbsp.	honey	45 mL
1/3 cup	unsalted butter	80 mL
1 tsp.	sea salt	5 mL
1/2 tsp.	black pepper	2.5 mL
1 Tbsp.	fresh thyme leaves	15 mL
2	bulbs fennel, tops removed, cut into 8 wedges, keeping the core intact	2
2	parsnips, peeled and cut into 1-inch (2.5-cm) pieces	2
1 lb.	butternut squash, peeled and cut into 1-inch (2.5-cm) cubes	454 g
2	carrots, peeled and cut into 1-inch (2.5-cm) pieces	2

Preheat the oven to 400°F (200°C). Melt the honey and butter together in a small pot. Add the salt, pepper and thyme.

Toss the prepared vegetables together in a bowl with the melted butter mixture. Spread the vegetables loosely on a baking sheet and roast in the upper third of the oven for 20–25 minutes, or until tender when tested with a fork.

Plate Size

A large plate makes a small portion more dramatic. Run your extended finger from the outside of the rim towards the centre; if the finger touches the food, the plate is overfilled. And by the way, those little wooden bowls from salad sets should be sold at garage sales, or used in the bathroom as soap dishes. My rule: never serve any course on a plate smaller than your head!

—Glenys Morgan

Green Chickpea "Ratatouille"

*This is somewhat like a vegetable Sloppy Joe. Some of the eggplant
disintegrates into the sauce and gives it a luxurious taste and texture. It
can be eaten as is, with some bread, or spooned over rice, bulgur, pasta
or Creamy Polenta with Mushrooms and Leeks (page 87). Cold,
it makes a delicious wrapped sandwich.*

Serves 4 to 6		Karen Barnaby
2 lbs.	eggplant, peeled and cut into 1-inch (2.5-cm) slices	900 g
	extra virgin olive oil for broiling	
2 Tbsp.	extra virgin olive oil	30 mL
1 cup	onion, cut into 1/4-inch (.6-cm) dice	240 mL
4	cloves garlic, minced	4
1	28-oz. (796-mL) can plum tomatoes, drained and finely chopped	1
1/4 tsp.	ground cinnamon	1.2 mL
1	19-oz. (540-mL) can chickpeas, drained and rinsed	1
6 cups	water	1.5 L
2 lbs.	spinach, washed, trimmed and finely chopped	900 g
	salt and freshly ground black pepper to taste	
12	leaves fresh basil, torn into pieces	12

Preheat the broiler. Brush the eggplant on both sides with olive oil and place
on a rimmed baking sheet. Broil close to the heat, turning once, until tender
and lightly browned on both sides. Let cool and cut each slice into quarters.

Heat the 2 Tbsp. (30 mL) olive oil in a large pot over medium heat. Add the
onion and cook until translucent. Add the garlic and cook for a minute
longer. Add the tomatoes, cinnamon and chickpeas. Bring to a boil and add
the water and eggplant.

Cook at a lively simmer for 20 minutes, stirring occasionally. By this point,
the mixture should be thick but still fluid. Stir in the spinach and simmer for
10 minutes longer. Season with salt and pepper. Stir in the basil and remove
from the heat. Serve immediately.

Asian Green Beans

Fast and easy. Use tender green beans—I like haricots vert.
If the beans are larger, you can blanch them ahead to reduce the
cooking time.

Serves 4 to 6		Deb Connors
2 Tbsp.	oil	30 mL
1	clove garlic, chopped	1
1/2	red onion, peeled and cut in fine julienne	1/2
1/2 lb.	green beans	227 g
1/2	red bell pepper, seeds and membrane removed, cut in fine julienne	1/2
1/2	yellow bell pepper, seeds and membrane removed, cut in fine julienne	1/2
2 Tbsp.	sugar	30 mL
2 Tbsp.	light soy sauce	30 mL
	pinch of dried chili flakes	
	salt to taste	

Heat the oil in a large sauté pan over medium-high heat. Sauté the garlic and red onion for 1 minute. Add the green beans and red and yellow peppers. Sprinkle with the sugar, soy sauce, chilies and salt. Sauté for 3–4 minutes, or until the beans are tender.

• • • • • •
Quick Fix:

Santorini's Feta Tomatoes

Cut a medium tomato in half horizontally and scoop out the seeds. Mix together some feta, ricotta and mayonnaise. Season to taste with salt and pepper. Spoon it onto the tomato halves and bake in a preheated 350°F (175°C) oven for 15–20 minutes. Garnish with chives.

—Lesley Stowe

Braised Bok Choy with Mustard Seeds and Chilies

As a change of pace from stir-frying, the bok choy in this recipe is cooked beyond crispness into a state of silkiness. This also works well with gai lan, sui choy or Chinese mustard greens. Serve it with Red-Cooked Lamb Shanks with Star Anise and Ginger (page 110).

Serves 4		Karen Barnaby
2 lbs.	baby bok choy or baby Shanghai bok choy	900 g
2 Tbsp.	vegetable oil	30 mL
1 Tbsp.	black mustard seeds	15 mL
4	cloves garlic, thinly sliced	4
3	dried hot chili peppers	3
1/4 tsp.	salt	1.2 mL
1/4 tsp.	sugar	1.2 mL

Remove any yellow outer leaves from the bok choy. Cut them in half lengthwise and wash by running water between the stems to remove any dirt. Turn it upside down in a colander to drain for 30 minutes.

Heat the vegetable oil in a heavy pot over high heat. Add the mustard seeds. As soon as they begin to pop, remove the pan from the heat and add the garlic and chilies. Stir for a moment, then return to the heat and add the bok choy, stirring rapidly to coat it with the oil. Continue stirring until the bok choy reduces in bulk and starts to exude water. Add the salt and sugar. Turn the heat to low and cover with a lid. Braise for 10 minutes, stirring occasionally. If a lot of water is left in the pan at the end of cooking, turn the heat to high and stir frequently until the water has almost evaporated.

Steady Chopping

I always place a damp kitchen towel under my cutting board so it will not slide around while I am chopping.

—Mary Mackay

Après-Ski Skillet of Potatoes, Peppers and Feta

This is as close as I come to a favourite, after-work, quick-fix meal and it is also a favourite after a day of cross-country skiing. It fits the criteria—quick, easy and satisfying. I almost always have these ingredients on hand, and if not I substitute. It also makes a great accompaniment to any simple roasted meat or chicken.

Serves 4		Margaret Chisholm
1 Tbsp.	olive oil	15 mL
1	clove garlic, chopped	1
1	medium onion, sliced	1
2	red bell peppers, sliced	2
3	large red-skinned potatoes, thinly sliced	3
	salt and freshly ground black pepper to taste	
3	tomatoes, sliced	3
1 tsp.	fresh thyme	5 mL
8 oz.	feta cheese, crumbled	227 g

Preheat the oven to 375°F (190°C).

Heat the olive oil over medium heat in a 10- to 12-inch (24- to 30-cm) cast-iron frying pan or other heavy ovenproof skillet. Add the garlic and onion and sauté for 2 or 3 minutes. Add the peppers and stir and cook for 2 minutes. Add the potatoes in layers, sprinkling with salt and pepper as you go. Add the tomatoes and thyme. Season with salt and pepper. Sprinkle with feta. Cook on top of the stove for 4 or 5 minutes.

Transfer the pan to the oven and bake for 35 minutes, or until the potatoes are tender.

Smoked Gruyère Potato Casserole

These potatoes are a nice side dish with the BBQ Back Ribs (page 106).
You can substitute sliced provolone for the grated Cheddar cheese and
regular Gruyère for the smoked.

Serves 8 to 10		Deb Connors
3 lbs.	baking potatoes, peeled and cut into 1-inch (2.5-cm) cubes	1.4 kg
1 cup	whipping cream	240 mL
1/2 cup	sun-dried tomatoes, tightly packed, chopped	120 mL
4	shallots, peeled and minced	4
2 Tbsp.	chopped basil	30 mL
1 cup	grated smoked Gruyère cheese	240 mL
1 tsp.	salt	5 mL
1 tsp.	freshly ground black pepper	5 mL
1/2 cup	grated white Cheddar cheese	120 mL

Preheat the oven to 350ºF (175ºC).

Cook the potatoes in boiling, salted water until they are almost fully cooked.
In a large bowl, combine the cream, sun-dried tomatoes, shallot, basil,
Gruyère, salt and pepper. Add the potatoes and mix thoroughly until the
liquid has been absorbed by the potatoes.

Butter and line a 10- x 10-inch (25- x 25-cm) baking pan with parchment
paper. Place the potato mixture in the pan, smoothing and pressing it down
with a rubber spatula. Cover the pan with parchment paper and then
aluminum foil. Bake for 50 minutes. Remove the foil and parchment paper
and top with the grated Cheddar cheese. Return it to the oven for a few
minutes to melt the Cheddar cheese.

Sun-Dried Tomatoes

Reconstitute sun-dried tomatoes by
soaking them in boiling water for
30–60 seconds. This will make the
tomatoes much easier to chop or
julienne. You can save the water for
flavouring soups or sauces.

—Deb Connors

Honey and Thyme Roasted Winter Vegetables (page 79).

Jerk Chicken with Cucumber Lime Salsa (page 95).

Grilled Portobello and Steak with Asian Marinade (page 108).

Halibut and "Chips" (page 115)
and Golden Oven Fries (page 86).

Grilled Prawns with
Smoked Pepper Tartar Sauce
(page 128).

Award-winning Biscotti Pears
with Caramel Sauce (page 142).

*Banana Chocolate Chiffon
Cake with Bourbon Cream
(page 164).*

Crispy Chocolate and Black
Pepper Shortbread (page 175)
Chocolate Truffles (page 171)
and Lemon Meringue Kisses
(page 167).

Horseradish Mashed Potatoes with Spinach

This combination of vegetables makes a great bed for a simple fish dish or roasted beef. If you can find fresh horseradish, your dish will have a spirited zing.

Serves 6		Margaret Chisholm
1/4 cup	shallots, chopped	60 mL
1/4 cup	water	60 mL
1 Tbsp.	unsalted butter	15 mL
1/2 tsp.	salt	2.5 mL
14 cups	spinach leaves	3.5 L
3 lbs.	Yukon Gold potatoes	1.4 kg
2 tsp.	salt	10 mL
3 Tbsp.	unsalted butter	45 mL
1 cup	hot milk	240 mL
	salt and freshly ground black pepper to taste	
4–6 Tbsp.	freshly grated or prepared horseradish	60–90 mL

Place the shallots, water, 1 Tbsp. (15 mL) butter and 1/2 tsp. (2.5 mL) salt in a large saucepan. Bring to a boil, then reduce to a simmer. Simmer for 2 minutes. Set aside to cool for a few minutes. Place the spinach on top of this mixture. Set aside.

Peel the potatoes and cut each into 8 pieces. Place in a medium saucepan and cover with cold water and the 2 tsp. (10 mL) salt. Bring to a boil and cook over medium heat for approximately 20 minutes, or until the potatoes are tender. Drain in a colander and return the potatoes to the pot. Place over low heat and toss the pan a few times to dry them out. One or two minutes should be plenty.

Put the potatoes through a potato ricer or mash them with a potato masher. Return them to the pot. Beat in the 3 Tbsp. (45 mL) butter in small pieces, using a wooden spoon. Beat in the hot milk. Season with salt and pepper. Stir in the horseradish. Cover and keep warm.

Place the pot of spinach over high heat. Bring it to a boil and reduce the heat to medium. Stir and simmer for 1 minute, or until the spinach is just wilted. Remove from the heat. To serve, spoon a mound of potatoes on each plate and top with a mound of spinach.

Golden Oven Fries

It's hard to believe that these potatoes are not deep-fried. They have all the crispness and browning of their deep-fried cousins but without the guilt and fat. When you are choosing potatoes, remember that the old russets brown much better than new potatoes. Save the young potatoes for salads and steaming.

Serves 6		*Caren McSherry-Valagao*
8	large russet potatoes	8
1/3 cup	good-quality olive oil	80 mL
	sea salt and freshly ground black pepper to taste	

Preheat the oven to 425°F (220°C). Peel the potatoes if you don't like the skin. Cut them into lengthwise strips, not too skinny, not too thick.

Place the potatoes in a single layer on a baking sheet and drizzle with the olive oil. Rub them with your hands so that they are evenly coated on all sides. Sprinkle with salt and pepper. Bake them for about 40 minutes, turning them occasionally.

Food Scissors

I reserve a "food only" pair of scissors for chopping sticky things like sun-dried tomatoes, figs, apricots or any food that sticks to a knife. The sticky foods never stick to the scissors. Be very careful that the scissors that bear the name KITCHEN do not find their way to the garage for the chores or with the kids to the craft room.

—Caren McSherry-Valagao

Creamy Polenta with Mushrooms and Leeks

To stir or not to stir, that is the question. Polenta can be prepared in the oven or on the stovetop. When roasting meats the oven temperature is often too hot for polenta, so I use the stovetop method, which requires some time and patience. I cut back on time by using regular yellow cornmeal. It results in a smooth stick-to-your-ribs corn porridge. If you are willing to spend a bit more time at the stove, use stone-ground cornmeal. It requires about 35 minutes of stirring and gives a grainier texture. Polenta is a heavy dish and a little goes a long way. If you have leftovers, spread the polenta out flat on an oiled baking sheet and refrigerate overnight. Next morning slice up the polenta, fry it in a little olive oil and serve it with eggs.

Serves 4		Mary Mackay
2 cups	chicken stock	475 mL
1 cup	water	240 mL
2/3 cup	yellow cornmeal	160 mL
2 Tbsp.	unsalted butter	30 mL
1 1/2 cups	sliced mushrooms, preferably shiitake	360 mL
3/4 cup	diced leeks, white part only	180 mL
1/4 cup	dry white wine	60 mL
3 Tbsp.	grated Parmesan cheese	45 mL
	sea salt and freshly cracked black pepper to taste	

Bring the chicken stock and water to a boil on high heat in a heavy saucepan. Slowly whisk in the cornmeal. Reduce the heat to medium-low and cook for 15 minutes, stirring often.

While the polenta is cooking, prepare the mushrooms and leeks. Heat 1 Tbsp. (15 mL) of the butter in a large frying pan on medium-high heat. Add the mushrooms and leeks and sauté for 4 minutes. Add the white wine. Reduce the heat to medium-low and cook another 7 minutes. Keep the mushrooms and leeks warm until the polenta is fully cooked.

Stir the remaining 1 Tbsp. (15 mL) butter and Parmesan cheese into the cooked polenta. Stir in the mushrooms and leeks. Season with salt and pepper. Serve immediately in warm bowls.

Toasted Coconut Rice with Spice and Raisins

For some, cooking from a recipe without tweaking is hard to resist. I vowed authenticity when given a traditional Indian cookbook, but with an error in translation, I happily added three cups of coconut to the dish. I'm back to tweaking and this pilaf is the result. It cooks quickly and is lighter than those made with coconut milk. Serve it with Grilled Portobello and Steak in Asian Marinade (page 108), Turkey Breast with Chipotle Bourbon Cranberry Sauce (page 102) or a quick curry made with one of the good commercial pastes.

Serves 4 to 6		Glenys Morgan
1 1/2 cups	basmati rice	360 mL
1/2 cup	desiccated unsweetened coconut	120 mL
2	green chiles, seeded and minced	2
1 tsp.	salt	5 mL
1 tsp.	sugar	5 mL
1/4 cup	golden raisins	60 mL
2	bay leaves	2
1	cinnamon stick	1
4	whole cardamom pods	4
4 Tbsp.	butter	60 mL
2 1/2 cups	milk (low-fat and skim are fine)	600 mL
1 1/4 cups	water	300 mL

Combine the rice with the coconut, chiles, salt, sugar, raisins, bay leaves, cinnamon stick, and cardamom. Heat the butter in a large saucepan over medium heat. Add the rice mixture and sauté over medium heat for 5 minutes, stirring constantly. The coconut will toast to a golden colour, which adds to the nutty flavour; be careful not to burn it.

Add the milk and water and increase the heat to high. Bring the rice to a boil, stir and reduce the heat to low. Cover and cook for about 20 minutes, until the liquid has evaporated and holes have appeared in the surface. Fluff with a fork, remove the cinnamon stick and bay leaves and serve.

Jalapeño Cornbread

A great accompaniment for BBQ Back Ribs (page 106), this can also be made in muffin tins, or the little cast-iron individual cornbread molds.

Makes one 9- x 5-inch (23- x 13-cm) loaf pan		Deb Connors
1 cup	all-purpose flour	240 mL
1 cup	yellow cornmeal	240 mL
6 Tbsp.	sugar	90 mL
1/2 tsp.	salt	2.5 mL
1/4 tsp.	white pepper	1.2 mL
1 Tbsp.	baking powder	15 mL
1 cup	milk	240 mL
2	large eggs, beaten	2
1/4 cup	melted butter	60 mL
1/4 tsp.	hot pepper sauce	1.2 mL
1 Tbsp.	chopped parsley	15 mL
1 Tbsp.	chopped cilantro	15 mL
1	jalapeño, finely diced	1

Preheat the oven to 350°F (180°C). Lightly oil and flour a 9- x 5-inch (23- x 13-cm) loaf pan.

In a medium bowl, sift together the flour, cornmeal, sugar, salt, pepper and baking powder.

In a separate bowl whisk together the milk, beaten eggs, melted butter and hot pepper sauce. Stir in the parsley, cilantro and jalapeño. Add the dry ingredients and mix together.

Pour the batter into the prepared loaf pan and bake for 30 minutes. Turn out onto a rack and let cool.

Entrées

Breast of Chicken with Morels and Cranberries

I love serving this recipe as soon as fresh cranberries hit the market.
The contrast of the rich morel sauce and tangy cranberries is fabulous.
Try to use free-range chicken—the difference in flavour and texture
is worth the higher price.

Serves 6		Lesley Stowe
3 oz.	dried morels	85 g
1/3 cup	olive oil	80 mL
1/2 cup	shallots, finely chopped	120 mL
1 cup	cranberries	240 mL
2 1/2 cups	port	600 mL
1 Tbsp.	julienned orange rind	15 mL
3	whole boneless chicken breasts, halved	3
6 cups	chicken stock, reduced by half	1.5 L
	juice of 2 oranges	
	salt and freshly ground black pepper to taste	

Soak the morels in warm water for 15–20 minutes until softened. Rinse and rub gently to remove any dirt. Drain and pat dry. Cut them in half lengthwise.

Heat half the olive oil in a sauté pan and sauté the shallots until soft, 3–5 minutes. Add the morels and cook 5 minutes more. Add the cranberries and 1/3 cup (80 mL) of the port. Simmer for 5 minutes. Add the orange rind and remove from the heat.

Preheat the oven to 375°F (190°C). Heat the remaining olive oil in a sauté pan over medium-high heat and cook the chicken breasts in batches until lightly browned on each side, about 2 minutes per side. Remove the chicken to a 9- x 13-inch (23- x 33-cm) ovenproof dish that will hold the chicken in one layer, and finish cooking in the oven for 10–15 minutes.

Pour off the fat from the sauté pan and blot any remaining fat with paper towel. Add the chicken stock, remaining port and orange juice to the sauté pan; stir over medium-high heat, scraping up any browned bits. Boil until it is reduced enough to coat the back of a spoon. Season with salt and pepper. Place one chicken breast on each plate and spoon the sauce over each serving. Garnish with orange rind.

Chicken Marengo

*This is one of the first dishes I learned to make at the Dubrulle
Culinary School. I still enjoy its simplicity and combination of flavours.
Marengo is a dish of veal or chicken sautéed in olive oil and cooked in
tomatoes, onions, olives, garlic and white wine. Traditionally garnished
with fried eggs and crayfish, I prefer to serve Chicken Marengo
with steamed rice or Fennel Mashed Potatoes (The Girls
Who Dish, page 126).*

Serves 4		Mary Mackay
2	whole boneless skinless chicken breasts, halved, rinsed and patted dry	2
	sea salt and freshly cracked black pepper to taste	
2 Tbsp.	olive oil	30 mL
1 cup	diced onion	240 mL
1	large portobello mushroom, diced	1
12	cultivated white mushrooms, cut in half	12
1 Tbsp.	minced garlic	15 mL
1/2 tsp.	sea salt	2.5 mL
1/2 cup	dry white wine	120 mL
1	28-oz. (796-mL) can plum tomatoes	1
24	green olives, pitted	24
1 Tbsp.	chopped fresh sage	15 mL
	freshly cracked black pepper to taste	

Preheat the oven to 400°F (200°C).

Cut each chicken breast into three pieces. Season the chicken with salt
and pepper. Heat the olive oil in a large frying pan over medium-high heat.
Add the chicken pieces and brown for 2 minutes on each side. Transfer the
chicken to an 8-cup (2-L) ovenproof casserole dish. Add the onion and
mushrooms to the frying pan and sauté for 4 minutes until soft. Add the
garlic and salt and cook for 1 minute more. Stir in the white wine, tomatoes,
olives and sage and bring to a full boil. Pour the tomato mixture over top of
the chicken and cover with a lid.

Place the casserole dish on a baking sheet. Bake until the chicken is cooked
through, about 20–30 minutes. Season the dish with pepper. The chicken can
be served directly out of the casserole dish or transferred to a warm platter.

Sauté of Chicken with Gorgonzola and Fresh Herbs

Plump free-range chicken breasts are a delight in a dish like this. Removing the skin lowers the fat but keeping the bone adds flavour and keeps the meat moist. I use the milder Gorgonzola dolce from my Italian grocer but occasionally I get a delicious true Roquefort, which is sheep's milk, from Lesley Stowe's wonderful selection of cheeses. For a lighter sauce, omit the cream, reduce the chicken stock to a glaze, and crumble the cheese in at the end. Serve with fluffy mashed potatoes, perhaps with extra chives folded in.

Serves 6		Glenys Morgan
3	whole bone-in skinless chicken breasts, halved	3
1/4 tsp.	salt	1.2 mL
	freshly ground white pepper to taste	
	flour for dredging	
2 Tbsp.	unsalted butter	30 mL
2 Tbsp.	olive oil	30 mL
1/2 cup	chicken stock, preferably homemade	120 mL
3 oz.	Gorgonzola or other blue cheese	85 g
1 cup	whipping cream	240 mL
2 Tbsp.	minced fresh tarragon	30 mL
2 Tbsp.	minced fresh chives	30 mL

Season the chicken breasts with salt and pepper and dredge with flour. Shake off the excess.

Heat the butter and oil in a skillet over medium-high heat; add the chicken when the foam subsides and sauté the breasts until golden, turning only once, 2–3 minutes per side. (The chicken will not be cooked through.) Reduce the heat to medium-low and add half the chicken stock. Cover and cook for 5 minutes, or until the chicken is cooked through. Transfer the chicken to a plate and keep warm.

Mash the Gorgonzola with 1/4 cup (60 mL) of the cream. Add the remaining chicken stock to the skillet. Cook over high heat, scraping until the sauce is reduced to a glaze. Add the remaining cream and cook, stirring, until reduced to 1/2 cup (120 mL).

Whisk in the Gorgonzola cream. Reduce the sauce over low heat until it coats the back of a spoon. Add the tarragon and chives. (The recipe may be prepared to this point up to 2 hours ahead.) Add the chicken breasts to the sauce, cover and cook over low heat until just heated through. To serve, transfer to plates and spoon the sauce on top.

Jerk Chicken with Cucumber Lime Salsa

This spicy, sweet chicken from the Caribbean is delicious hot or cold with the cooling salsa. I make it with chicken thighs because of their richer flavour, but it works equally well with boneless skinless breasts. Serve with Cumin-Roasted Yams (The Girls Who Dish, page 127).

Serves 4		Margaret Chisholm
1/2 cup	chopped onion	120 mL
3	green onions, chopped	3
1 tsp.	ground allspice	5 mL
1 Tbsp.	dried thyme	15 mL
1/2 tsp.	cayenne pepper	2.5 mL
1 tsp.	freshly ground black pepper	5 mL
3/4 tsp.	each ground nutmeg and ground cinnamon	4 mL
2 tsp.	each salt and sugar	10 mL
2	cloves garlic, chopped	2
1–2	jalepeño peppers, chopped	1–2
12	boneless skinless chicken thighs	12
1 recipe	Cucumber Lime Salsa (page 96)	1 recipe

Grind all ingredients except the chicken to a fine paste in the food processor. (You may keep this mixture covered in the refrigerator for up to 2 weeks.) Poke each piece of chicken with the tip of a sharp knife to make 1/2-inch (1.2-cm) slits in 8 or 10 places; this allows the marinade to penetrate the chicken. Toss the chicken with the jerk paste and marinate for 2–3 hours in the refrigerator. Grill or barbecue the chicken over medium heat on a preheated barbecue for 10–12 minutes, or until it's cooked through. Serve with Cucumber Lime Salsa.

Cucumber Lime Salsa

One key to making this cooling, slightly sweet salsa is to very finely dice the cucumbers and onions.

Makes 2 cups (475 mL)

1/2	long English cucumber, cut into 1/4-inch (.6-cm) dice	1/2
2 Tbsp.	freshly squeezed lime juice	30 mL
2 Tbsp.	extra virgin olive oil	30 mL
3 Tbsp.	finely chopped red onion	45 mL
1/3 cup	chopped cilantro	80 mL
1 1/2 Tbsp.	chopped mint	22.5 mL
	salt and freshly ground black pepper to taste	
2 tsp.	sugar	10 mL

Combine all the ingredients in a bowl and marinate for 1 hour. Serve chilled.

Secret

I swore that when I had children they would never be the product of fast food or packaged dinners. When my daughter was about four she went to a friend's house after preschool. Upon returning home, she declared that the friend's mom made the best macaroni and cheese in the world. I questioned her with intensity—better than mommy's and gramma's? Her reply was an emphatic yes! This one came from a box and she got to sprinkle the little packet of cheese over. Two years passed before I finally gave in to the demand. Whenever the occasion to make that dinner arises, I can't wait to dive in myself. It is pretty darn good, although I would never admit to it.

—Caren McSherry-Valagao

Crunchy Baked "Tempura" Lemon Chicken

Imagine two sisters: one lives to cook and the other cooks to live. In the busiest of times, my working-mom sister maintains the ritual of gathering for a meal—not as a culinary exercise but a recipe for well-fed bodies and souls. My sister Lorrie's version of this is even simpler—she uses boneless skinless chicken breasts and regular bread crumbs. The chicken is perfectly cooked in about 20 minutes.

Serves 4		Glenys Morgan
4 Tbsp.	butter	60 mL
3	lemons	3
2 cups	panko (Japanese bread crumbs)	475 mL
1/4 cup	Dijon mustard	60 mL
2	whole bone-in skinless chicken breasts, halved, preferably free-range	2

Preheat the oven to 400°F (200°C). Line a baking pan with foil. Melt the butter on the baking pan in the oven while preparing the chicken.

Grate the zest from the lemons and add it to the bread crumbs. Combine the juice from the lemons with the mustard and dip the chicken breasts to coat. Roll in the panko and place bone side down on the baking sheet.

Bake about 30 minutes, until the chicken is firm and a paring knife slides into the meat like a perfectly cooked potato. The blade should feel "too hot" on the back of the hand. Serve hot or at room temperature.

Deep Dish Chicken Phyllo Tart

This recipe doubles as a light dinner entrée or a great luncheon dish. It partners well with most foods and usually steals the show on a buffet table. Don't be afraid to tackle the phyllo pastry; just remember, it dries out quickly, so leave the telephone to answer itself once the package is open. You can use jarred roasted peppers in this recipe. Freeze leftover phyllo sheets in a sealed plastic bag for another use.

Serves 8 to 10		Caren McSherry-Valagao
1	large bunch fresh spinach, stemmed	1
2 Tbsp.	good-quality olive oil	30 mL
3	large leeks, white part only, finely sliced	3
1 cup	long-grain rice	240 mL
2 cups	water	475 mL
1	large egg	1
1 cup	half-and-half cream	240 mL
2 Tbsp.	chopped fresh dill	30 mL
1 Tbsp.	chopped fresh thyme	30 mL
1/2 lb.	feta cheese, crumbled	227 g
2/3 cup	oil-packed sun-dried tomatoes, drained and chopped	160 mL
2 cups	cooked chicken meat, diced	475 mL
1 cup	kalamata olives, pitted and chopped	240 mL
	sea salt and freshly ground black pepper to taste	
1	package phyllo pastry, thawed	1
3	red bell peppers, roasted and peeled	3

Steam the spinach and refresh in cold water. Squeeze out all the moisture. Finely chop it and set aside.

In a small pot heat the olive oil; add the leek and sauté until soft. Stir in the rice and cook for about 2 minutes. Pour in the water, cover and bring to a boil. Reduce to a simmer and cook until the rice is tender and the water has evaporated, about 10 minutes. Set aside. Preheat the oven to 375°F (190°C).

In a large bowl beat the egg. Add the cream, dill, thyme, feta cheese, sun-dried tomatoes, chicken, olives, cooked rice and spinach. Season with salt and pepper. Stir well to combine and set aside.

Have ready a 10-inch (25-cm) springform pan. Place one sheet of phyllo dough on your work surface and brush it lightly with olive oil. (Cover the rest with a slightly damp cloth.) Fold the sheet in half and place the end of the dough in the centre of the pan, leaving half the sheet hanging over the edge of the pan. Repeat this process, overlapping each sheet by about 2 inches (5 cm) until you have covered the entire pan. You will use about 10 or 12 sheets in total.

Pour half the filling into the pan, spreading it evenly. Place the red peppers over the filling in a single layer and spread the remaining half of the filling over the peppers. Fold the overhanging phyllo sheets back over the tart, covering the filling. It gives an interesting finish if you twist the phyllo when folding it back. Bake for about 30 minutes, or until the pastry is golden brown.

• • • • • •
Quick Fix:

Boursin Chicken

Stuff approximately 1 Tbsp. (15 mL) Boursin herb cheese under the skin of each boneless chicken breast you're serving. Season the skin with salt and pepper and bake in a preheated 350°F (175°C) oven for 30 minutes.

—Lesley Stowe

Cornish Game Hens Stuffed with Olives and Thyme

Stuffing a paste of black olives between the breast meat and the skin gives the meat extra flavour and moisture. I like to serve these roasted hens over a scoop of Creamy Polenta with Mushrooms and Leeks (page 87). If you are having a large meal, cut the recipe in half and serve half a hen per person.

Serves 4		Mary Mackay
1 cup	green olives, pitted (about 40 small olives)	240 mL
1 cup	kalamata olives, pitted (about 40 olives)	240 mL
6	cloves garlic	6
2 tsp.	capers	10 mL
2 Tbsp.	chopped parsley	30 mL
3 Tbsp.	chopped fresh thyme	45 mL
1 tsp.	finely chopped orange zest	5 mL
3 Tbsp.	olive oil	45 mL
4	1 1/4-lb. (565-g) Cornish game hens, giblets removed	4
1 tsp.	olive oil	5 mL
	sea salt and freshly cracked black pepper to taste	
1	lemon, cut in quarters	1
1 Tbsp.	chopped fresh thyme	15 mL
1/2 cup	dry white wine	120 mL

Preheat the oven to 450°F (230°C).

Place the olives, garlic, capers, parsley, the 3 Tbsp. (45 mL) fresh thyme and orange zest in the bowl of a food processor. Using the steel knife attachment, pulse the mixture for a few seconds, until it is chunky. Add the 3 Tbsp. (45 mL) olive oil and pulse a few seconds longer until puréed. Stop before it gets totally smooth; it should be slightly chunky. Divide the olive paste into 4 portions and set aside.

Rinse the Cornish game hens under water and pat dry with paper towel. Starting from the cavity, use your fingers to gently loosen the skin from the meat. Slide a portion of olive paste under the skin of the breast and leg meat, spreading it over the meat as evenly as possible. Be careful not to break open the skin when stuffing. Rub the skins with the 1 tsp. (5 mL) olive oil. Season the inside cavity and outside of the hens with salt and pepper. Place a wedge of lemon inside each hen. Tie the legs together and tuck the wing tips under the hens. Sprinkle the remaining 1 Tbsp. (15 mL) fresh thyme over top of the hens.

Place the hens on a rack in a large roasting pan and roast for 15 minutes. Pour off any oil that has collected on the bottom of the pan. If your oven gets a little smoky like mine, add some water to the bottom of the roasting pan. Lower the oven temperature to 400°F (200°C) and bake until the juices run clear when the thickest part of the thigh is pierced with a paring knife, about 40–45 minutes. Transfer the hens to a platter.

Pour the pan juices into a container and set aside. Place the roasting pan over medium-high heat, add the white wine and simmer while scraping the bottom of the pan with a spatula. Spoon off the fat from the reserved pan juices and add the juices to the roasting pan. Simmer for 3 minutes, then strain. To serve, pour some juice over each hen.

Testing Herbs

If you're seized by the fear of trying a new herb or spice, take a hint from the Italians tasting olive oil. If you've never used it before, add some to a batch of steamed potatoes, season simply with salt (preferably sea salt) and pepper, and add some butter or olive oil. Discover the herb's personality. If I think a spice or herb smells sweet, my favourite experiment is to add a little to an apple pie or simmer it in some applesauce (canned will do nicely) to serve with pancakes or pork. On a recent adventure I tucked kaffir lime leaves into a pie. The apple-lime combo is now a favourite.

—Glenys Morgan

Turkey Breast with Chipotle Bourbon Cranberry Sauce

When celebrations with turkey centre-stage roll around, phone calls begin coming in for this sweet and spicy cranberry sauce. Each ingredient contributes a distinctive touch but I especially like the star anise and bourbon together. No one ever expects the heat and smokiness from the chipotle. The turkey saté is delicious but was really just an excuse to get the sauce in print, keeping the lost recipe calls at bay. If turkey isn't a favourite, use the saté paste on lamb, chicken or pork tenderloin. Kecap manis is a thick Indonesian sauce available in Asian markets; substitute soy if you wish.

Serves 6 to 8		Glenys Morgan
1	small onion, peeled and quartered	1
1	lime or lemon, juice only	1
1/2 cup	natural peanut butter, preferably chunky style	120 mL
2	cloves garlic, minced	2
2 tsp.	ground coriander	10 mL
2 tsp.	ground cumin	10 mL
1 Tbsp.	sambal oelek or Thai chili sauce	15 mL
1/4 cup	kecap manis or soy sauce	60 mL
1 Tbsp.	brown sugar	15 mL
1	2-lb. (900-g) boneless turkey breast	1

To quickly assemble the saté paste, combine all the ingredients except the turkey in the food processor and blend to a crunchy paste. If working it by hand, the onion must be very finely minced before combining the ingredients for the paste.

Coat the outside of the turkey breast with the paste and wrap the breast in plastic wrap. To keep the paste on the turkey when removing the plastic wrap, spray it first with vegetable spray. Marinate in the refrigerator for up to 24 hours. Remove from the refrigerator half an hour before cooking. This is delicious finished on the grill, so if your BBQ is suitable for roasts, follow the roasting instructions.

If you're baking it, preheat the oven to 425°F (220°C). Unwrap the turkey and reapply any of the paste that comes off. Roast the turkey for 15 minutes, then reduce the heat to 350°F (175°C). When it's perfectly cooked, the internal temperature at the thickest point should be 160°F (70°C) and will gain several more degrees when resting. Check the turkey after 30 minutes of roasting. Do not over- or undercook. Rest it for 10 minutes before slicing. Serve with the cranberry sauce on the side.

Chipotle Bourbon Cranberry Sauce

Makes about 2 cups (475 mL)

1	12-oz. (340-g) package cranberries, fresh or frozen	1
2 cups	apple juice or cider	500 mL
2	cinnamon sticks	2
4–6	clusters star anise (available in Asian food stores)	4–6
1 cup	dark brown sugar	250 mL
2–3	chipotle chiles in adobo sauce	2–3
1/4 cup	bourbon	60 mL
2	limes, juice only	2

In a non-reactive saucepan, combine the cranberries, juice or cider, cinnamon sticks and star anise pods. If you're unsure about how sweet the sauce will be, begin with 1/2 cup (120 mL) sugar. The rest may be added later to taste. Bring the berries to a boil, then reduce the heat to medium-low. The cranberries will cook completely in 20–30 minutes, bursting and turning the sauce deep red. In the last few minutes of cooking, taste for sugar and stir in more as desired. Remove from the heat and allow to cool slightly.

To make mincing the chiles easier, cut them on foil or parchment. After scraping the chiles into the pot, discard the paper. For a milder smoky flavour, omit the chipotles and spoon some of the adobo sauce into the cranberries. Add the bourbon and lime juice. The high natural pectin in cranberries keeps the sauce for months in the refrigerator.

Note: Chipotles in adobo are available in most grocery stores and specialty markets. Once the can has been opened they may be stored in a clean jar in the refrigerator or frozen to preserve their texture. Add to chili and salsa recipes for a pleasantly addictive smoky taste. Their heat dissipates as they're stored.

Veal Tenderloin with Blueberry Sauce and Sage Leaves

The mild flavour of veal lends itself well to the dried blueberries, but you could substitute chicken for the veal. Try to take the time to crisp the sage, because it really adds something to the finished dish. Serve it with Fennel Mashed Potatoes (The Girls Who Dish, page 126).

Serves 6		Lesley Stowe
1/4 cup	olive oil	60 mL
6	shallots, finely chopped	6
1 cup	dry red wine	240 mL
1/4 cup	dried blueberries	60 mL
2 cups	veal or chicken stock	475 mL
	pinch ground cinnamon	
1 1/2 Tbsp.	olive oil	22.5 mL
2 lbs.	pink veal tenderloin, sliced into 1/4-inch (.6-cm) medallions	900 g
	salt and freshly ground black pepper to taste	
1/2 cup	olive oil for deep frying	120 mL
32	small fresh sage leaves	32

In a sauté pan, heat the 1/4 cup (60 mL) olive oil over medium heat. Add the shallots and cook until they are soft but not brown. Add the wine, blueberries, 1 cup (240 mL) of the stock and the cinnamon. Reduce the heat to medium-low and let the mixture boil gently until it has reduced to approximately 1/2 cup (120 mL). Remove from the heat and set aside.

In a second sauté pan, heat the 1 1/2 Tbsp. (22.5 mL) olive oil and sauté the veal medallions over medium heat for approximately 2 minutes on each side. Place the veal on a serving platter and keep it warm. Pour off any excess oil from the pan and add the remaining 1 cup (240 mL) of stock. Scraping the pan to loosen any brown bits, allow the stock and veal juices to boil down to about 1/4 cup (60 mL). Add this reduced stock to the reserved blueberry sauce. Season to taste and keep warm.

While the stock is reducing, heat the 1/2 cup (120 mL) olive oil in a heavy pan to 325°F (165°C). When the oil is hot, add the sage leaves and cook for 1–2 minutes or until crispy. Remove with a slotted spoon and drain on paper towel. To serve, pour the blueberry sauce over the veal and garnish with the deep-fried sage leaves.

Pork Chops in a White Wine Game Marinade

Game marinades are usually made with red wine, but I wanted to keep the colour light to better complement the colour of the pork. Serve this on a chilly Sunday night with Honey and Thyme Roasted Winter Vegetables (page 79) and Horseradish Mashed Potatoes with Spinach (page 85).

Serves 4		Karen Barnaby
3 cups	white wine	720 mL
1/2 cup	each diced carrots, onions and celery	120 mL
1/4 cup	diced shallots	60 mL
1	clove garlic, sliced	1
1 tsp.	black peppercorns, coarsely crushed	5 mL
12	juniper berries, coarsely crushed	12
1/2 tsp.	salt	2.5 mL
4	pork loin chops, 9–11 oz. (250–300 g) each	4
2 tsp.	vegetable oil	10 mL
	salt and freshly ground black pepper to taste	

Combine the wine, carrot, onion, celery, shallots, garlic, peppercorns, juniper berries and salt in a non-corrodible pot. Bring to a boil, remove from the heat and cool completely. Place the pork chops in a non-corrodible container that will hold them snugly without overlapping. Pour the wine mixture over the pork, cover and refrigerate overnight.

Remove the pork from the marinade and strain the marinade into a bowl. Heat the vegetable oil in a frying pan over medium heat. Add the pork chops and scatter the vegetables and spices around them. Cook, turning the pork chops once, until they are richly browned on both sides. Add the marinade liquid, cover and cook over low heat, turning once, for 10–15 minutes.

Remove the pork chops to heated plates or a platter. Over high heat, reduce the sauce to 1 cup (240 mL). Strain the sauce, discarding the vegetables and herbs. Adjust the seasoning with salt and pepper, pour the sauce over the chops and serve.

BBQ Back Ribs

These ribs are a year-round favourite. They will win accolades at any potluck supper or family barbecue. The sauce and the rub are both do-ahead and the time in the oven will reduce the final cooking time to almost instant. Serve these ribs with Jalapeño Cornbread (page 89) and Bistro Slaw with Caramel Crunch Almonds (page 54).

Serves 4		Deb Connors

For the barbecue sauce:

1 cup	chili sauce	240 mL
1 cup	ketchup	240 mL
5 Tbsp.	steak sauce	75 mL
3 Tbsp.	Worcestershire sauce	45 mL
1 tsp.	hot pepper sauce	5 mL
2 Tbsp.	molasses	30 mL
1/2 cup	corn syrup	120 mL
1 cup	brown sugar	240 mL
1/4 cup	white wine vinegar	60 mL

Whisk all the ingredients together, mixing well so that all the sugar is dissolved. This sauce makes 3 1/2 cups (840 mL) and will keep for up to 2 weeks in the refrigerator.

For the rib rub:

1/4 cup	garlic salt	60 mL
1 1/2 tsp.	freshly ground white pepper	7.5 mL
1/2 cup	paprika	120 mL
1/4 cup	dry mustard	60 mL
1/4 cup	red wine vinegar	60 mL
1/4 cup	Worcestershire sauce	60 mL
1/2 cup	beer	120 mL

Combine all the ingredients and stir well to form a paste. This paste will keep indefinitely in the refrigerator.

To cook the ribs:

4	slabs of ribs, approximately 6 lbs. (2.7 kg)	4
	rib rub	
	barbecue sauce	

Preheat the oven to 300°F (140°C).

Brush the slabs on both sides with a generous amount of rib rub. Place the meat on one or two large rimmed baking trays in the oven. Add enough water to cover the bottom of the pan to a depth of 1/2 inch (1.2 cm). Cover tightly with aluminum foil and cook for 1 3/4 hours. Remove the ribs from the baking trays and coat liberally with the barbecue sauce. Let them cool.

You can finish the ribs on the barbecue, cooking them over medium heat for 5–10 minutes per side, basting often. Or put them in a 400°F (200°C) oven, baking for 10–15 minutes per side, basting often.

Secret Craving

For me, perogies fall in a category beyond mere craving—they are a way of life. They are a fixture in my freezer. Mostly I have them with a little half-and-half cream, salt, pepper and a grating of fresh nutmeg, but if I have a little basil or cilantro pesto handy, I relish the fancy flavour. I have recently discovered how delicious they are with rosemarino, a spicy substance from southern Italy. Most people will likely not enjoy it, but those who do will be passionate about it. It contains tiny fermented anchovies and lots of chilies. You will find it at serious purveyors of Italian goods.

—Margaret Chisholm

Grilled Portobello and Steak in Asian Marinade

*Meat eaters and vegetarians alike will enjoy this recipe by
diplomatically dividing the marinade between the two. Many times in
cooking classes the mushrooms win over the steak. Use resealable
plastic bags for marinating; the steak may be frozen in the bag and
thawed en route to an outdoor feast. When burgers are in order, tuck
the mushrooms into buns and slice the beef onto sourdough buns. For a
warm salad, thinly slice either or both over dark leafy greens. Boil the
marinade for a few minutes, strain and drizzle over the salad. For an
all-vegetable meal, omit the meat and use 4 large mushrooms.*

Serves 4 generously		Glenys Morgan
6	cloves garlic, minced or put through a press	6
1/2 cup	fresh ginger, peeled and grated, about a 4-inch (5-cm) piece of ginger root	120 mL
1/4 cup	kecap manis or soy sauce	60 mL
1/4 cup	sake or wine	60 mL
1/4 cup	rice wine vinegar or mirin	60 mL
1/4 cup	olive oil	60 mL
2 Tbsp.	sesame oil (I prefer Kadoya brand)	30 mL
1	flank steak, about 1 1/2 lbs. (680 g)	1
2	Portobello mushrooms, stem removed, about 4 inches (10 cm) across	2

In a large bowl or plastic bag, combine everything but the steak and
mushrooms. To save time preparing the marinade, or for larger batches, use a
blender, dropping the garlic and ginger in with the motor running. They will
grate without sticking to the blade. If there's no dietary restriction, the steak
and mushrooms may be marinated together. Otherwise divide the marinade
in two and proceed.

Marinate the steak for at least 1 hour at room temperature or longer
refrigerated. Marinate the mushrooms for 1 hour, turning frequently as they
absorb the marinade.

Let the meat return to room temperature before grilling. Heat the grill to very
hot. Scrape the excess marinade off the steak. Boil the marinade and reserve
for a dipping sauce if desired. Brush the grill with oil and grill the steaks

until nicely browned, turning once. Flank steak should be pink in the centre for the best flavour and texture. Let rest, loosely covered, for about 10 minutes before carving. Carve across the grain and at an angle, making the pieces wide but thin.

Place the mushrooms cap side down on an oiled grill. As the mushrooms cook, the juices will appear on top and then cook into the mushrooms. Turn to sear the underside of the caps. Serve whole or sliced into strips.

Curry-Crusted Leg of Lamb with Cumin Raita

This is a welcome change from the rosemary garlic rub everyone uses on lamb. Without much extra effort you get a taste of India. Serve with couscous or Toasted Coconut Rice with Spice and Raisins (page 88).

Serves 8 to 10		*Lesley Stowe*
1 Tbsp.	finely grated lemon zest	15 mL
1 Tbsp.	ground coriander	15 mL
1 tsp.	cayenne	5 mL
2 tsp.	ground cumin	10 mL
1/2 tsp.	turmeric	2.5 mL
3	cloves garlic, minced	3
2 Tbsp.	extra virgin olive oil	30 mL
1 tsp.	sea salt	5 mL
1/2 tsp.	black pepper	2.5 mL
1	4-lb. (1.8-kg) butterflied leg of lamb	1
1 recipe	Cumin Raita (page 110)	1 recipe

Mix everything but the lamb together to form a paste and rub it over the leg of lamb. Place the lamb on a platter, loosely cover and refrigerate, preferably overnight but at least 2 hours. Return the lamb to room temperature before cooking it.

Preheat the oven to 375°F (190°C). Transfer the lamb to a roasting pan and roast 45 minutes to 1 hour, or until the internal temperature for rare reads 140°F (60°C). Let rest 10–15 minutes before carving. Serve the raita separately.

Cumin Raita

Makes 3 cups (720 mL)

1 cup	sour cream	240 mL
1 cup	yogurt	240 mL
1/2	English cucumber, seeded, grated and drained	1/2
1/2	jalapeño pepper, finely minced	1/2
1 tsp.	ground cumin	5 mL
2 tsp.	finely chopped cilantro	10 mL
	salt and freshly ground black pepper to taste	

Mix the sour cream and yogurt together until smooth. Add the remaining ingredients. Refrigerate until serving time.

Red-Cooked Lamb Shanks with Star Anise and Ginger

This is a recipe that grew out of a title. Red-Cooked Lamb Shanks sounded good in my head, and turned out to be very good on the taste buds. Red cooking is a Chinese braising technique that marries meat with sweet, salty and aromatic flavours. This dish will fill your kitchen with the warm fragrance of ginger and star anise as it cooks, which is reason enough to make it. Serve it with rice and Braised Bok Choy with Mustard Seeds and Chilies (page 82).

Serves 4 to 6		*Karen Barnaby*
4	lamb shanks, approximately 1 lb. (454 g) each	4
1 cup	light soy sauce	240 mL
1/2 cup	Chinese cooking wine or dry sherry	120 mL
1/2 cup	sugar	120 mL
1	whole star anise	1
1/2 lb.	ginger, peeled and cut into 1/2-inch (1.2-cm) pieces	227 g
1	4-inch (10-cm) cinnamon stick	1
2 tsp.	whole black peppercorns	10 mL

Preheat the oven to 300°F (150°C).

Place the lamb shanks in a pot that will hold them comfortably and cover with cold water by a few inches. Bring to a boil, then turn to a simmer and skim off any scum that rises to the top. Add the soy sauce, wine or sherry, sugar, star anise, ginger, cinnamon stick and peppercorns and return to a boil. Cover tightly and place in the oven. Check occasionally to see if the liquid is still covering the lamb, adding boiling water if needed. Cook for 2–3 hours, until the lamb is extremely tender.

Remove from the oven, uncover, and let the lamb cool completely in the cooking liquid. Remove the shanks and strain the cooking liquid. Reserve half the ginger and discard the cinnamon stick, peppercorns and star anise.

You may refrigerate the lamb in the liquid for up to 2 days. When you are ready to finish the recipe, remove the congealed fat. Slowly bring the liquid to a boil to gently heat the shanks through, then remove them. Boil the liquid over high heat until it is reduced to 1 1/2 cups (360 mL). (If you have not refrigerated the lamb overnight, skim any fat from the cooking liquid before bringing it to a boil.)

Place the reserved ginger in a food processor with a bit of the reduced cooking liquid. Pulse until the ginger is reduced to shreds. Add to the rest of the reduced cooking liquid. Spoon the liquid over and around the lamb shanks. Preheat the broiler or barbecue to medium. Broil or grill slowly, turning frequently, until crusty in spots and heated all the way through. Watch the lamb attentively—the sugar in the sauce can easily cause it to burn. Serve immediately.

Rack of Lamb with Sun-Dried Cherry Sauce

"The Best of Vine and Valley" is a popular class I developed to showcase the great crops produced in our area, including B.C.'s VQA wines. Get the combination right and Pinot Noir pairs well with sun-dried cherries and herbs and loves the complement of earthy roasted garlic and caramelized onion. My Caramelized Onion and Potato Gratin (The Girls Who Dish, page 120) became the perfect accompaniment.

Serves 4		Glenys Morgan
2	cloves garlic, minced	2
1/4 cup	Dijon mustard	60 mL
1/4 cup	minced fresh parsley	60 mL
2 Tbsp.	minced fresh rosemary	30 mL
1 Tbsp.	minced fresh thyme	15 mL
2 Tbsp.	olive oil	30 mL
2	racks of lamb, trimmed and frenched, about 1 lb. (454 g) each	2
	freshly ground black pepper to taste	
1 cup	sun-dried cherries, preferably a combination of sweet and sour varieties (or a mixture of sun-dried berries and Mission figs)	240 mL
2 cups	red wine	475 mL
1/2 cup	balsamic vinegar	120 mL
1/4 cup	brown sugar or maple syrup	60 mL
2 Tbsp.	cold unsalted butter or veal demi-glace	30 mL

Preheat the oven to 450°F (230°C).

Make a paste by combining the garlic, Dijon mustard, herbs and olive oil. Apply the coating to the round outside of the rack. The entire "loin" of meat attached to the ribs should be nicely coated. Pepper the outside of the meat.

Begin the sauce by combining the sun-dried cherries, wine, balsamic vinegar and brown sugar or maple syrup in a non-reactive saucepan. Bring to a boil, then reduce the heat and simmer. Watch that all the liquid does not evaporate. When nicely thickened, remove from the heat until the lamb is finished.

Choose a small pan for roasting that matches the size of the racks—a skillet works well. Place the two racks with the ribs pointing toward each other, then insert the ribs between each other as though they were interlocking fingers. Place in the preheated oven and roast for 10 minutes; reduce the heat to 350°F (175°C) and test after another 15 minutes. Testing with an instant-read thermometer will give perfect results. Remove the lamb when the thermometer reads 125–130°F (52–55°C). Let the finished lamb rest wrapped in foil for 10 minutes while finishing the sauce. This sets the juices.

If there's any nice brown bits in the lamb pan, whisk in some of the cherry sauce and deglaze the pan. By now the sauce should be syrupy and the cherries plumped. Taste for sugar; it should be sweet and sour. Add any juices that accumulated from the lamb while it was resting and reheat the sauce. Whisk in the butter or demi-glace to enrich the sauce and balance the acidity.

Slice in between each rib, separating the tiny chops. Serve with the rich dark sauce drizzled on lamb and plate.

Secret Craving

Perhaps my most odd food craving is peanut butter and molasses. I discovered this as a child, but I had to enjoy it out of sight of my brothers and sisters or suffer their endless teasing about my weird tastes. I start with white bread and spread it with the peanut butter first, then swirl molasses over top.

—Margaret Chisholm

Pomegranate Roast Lamb

*Pomegranate molasses is highly concentrated pure pomegranate juice.
You can find it in specialty shops that specialize in Middle Eastern
or Iranian foods. It is an amazingly tasty substance. Brush it on meats
or chicken, add it to balsamic vinaigrette for an intensely fruity
dressing or enjoy it in club soda as a spritzer. I love it with roast lamb,
served with Minted Feta Salad (page 55) and washed down with a big
juicy Merlot. My sous-chef and I had the culinary moment of our
summer the year we discovered this magical substance.*

Serves 4 or 5		Margaret Chisholm
2 lbs.	boneless leg of lamb	900 g
1 tsp.	sea salt	5 mL
2 tsp.	freshly ground black pepper	10 mL
1 Tbsp.	olive oil	15 mL
1/2 cup	pomegranate molasses	120 mL
1 1/2 cups	chicken or veal stock	360 mL
1 Tbsp.	cold unsalted butter	15 mL
	salt and freshly ground black pepper to taste	

Preheat the oven to 325°F (165°C).

If your lamb comes in one of those elastic nets, remove it. Trim the lamb of
any visible fat and tie it in 2 or 3 places with kitchen string. Or, of course,
you can have your butcher do all of this. Season with salt and pepper.

Heat the olive oil in an ovenproof skillet over medium-high heat. When it's
almost smoking, add the lamb. Sear for about one minute on each side.
Remove from the heat and brush generously with 1/4 cup (60 mL) of the
pomegranate molasses.

Place the skillet in the oven and roast the meat for approximately 25 minutes
or until it registers 150°F (65°C) on a meat thermometer. Transfer the lamb
to a warm plate. Cover loosely with foil and set in a warm place to rest for
8–10 minutes.

Add the stock to the roasting pan. Deglaze the pan, stirring over medium
heat until it's reduced to 1/3 cup (80 mL). Add the remaining 1/4 cup
(60 mL) pomegranate molasses to the pan and stir until dissolved and heated
through. Whisk in the cold butter. Season with a little salt and pepper. To
serve, slice the lamb in thin slices and drizzle with the sauce.

Halibut and "Chips"

A little bit cheeky and a whole lot good. I've contemplated using sour cream and onion flavoured chips, but haven't got around to it yet. One of the best things about this (besides eating it) is squishing the bag of potato chips to turn them into crumbs.

Makes 6 servings		Karen Barnaby
1/2 cup	prepared mayonnaise	120 mL
1 Tbsp.	Dijon mustard	15 mL
1/4 tsp.	garlic powder	1.2 mL
1 1/4 tsp.	lemon juice	6.2 mL
1	3 1/2-oz. (100-g) bag plain potato chips	1
1 cup	panko (Japanese-style bread crumbs)	240 mL
6	6-oz. (170-g) halibut fillets	6

Preheat the oven to 350°F (175°C).

Combine the mayonnaise, mustard, garlic powder and lemon juice in a shallow bowl. Mix well.

Coarsely crush the potato chips by squashing them in the bag. Add the panko and shake well. Spread out onto a plate. Dip the halibut fillets into the mayonnaise mixture, coating them on all sides. Dip all sides into the potato chip mixture, patting gently to help the coating adhere. Place in a single layer on a baking sheet and bake for 15–20 minutes, until the halibut is cooked through and the crust is golden brown. Serve with lemon wedges, cocktail sauce or malt vinegar.

Storing Cilantro

To store cilantro, cut the bottom stems from the bunch. Wash the leaves in cold water and shake them dry. Lay out a continuous sheet of 5–6 paper towels or a tea towel and spread the cilantro out on it in a nearly single layer. Roll it up like a jelly roll and lightly dampen the outside of the towel. Store in a plastic bag in the fridge. If you have a large bunch of cilantro, divide it in half and make two rolls. Your cilantro will stay fresh and green for at least 2 weeks.

—Karen Barnaby

Chili-Crusted Cod on a Bed of Braised Lentils

Lentils come in all sorts of colours and varieties. The lentil that is currently the darling of the continental kitchen is the lentil du Puy. It brags of French heritage, but in reality this lentil is grown in central Canada and shipped off to France to assume a new identity. It is then sent back to us in Canada bearing the new name and boasting of being a product of France. These lentils are a bit more money, but they produce a firmer, tastier final result. Go in search of a lentil bearing two nationalities. This dish looks attractive with roasted carrots or peppers on the side.

Serves 6		Caren McSherry-Valagao

For the lentils:

2 cups	lentil du Puy	475 mL
4 cups	water	950 mL
1	dry pasilla chili	1
2 Tbsp.	good-quality olive oil	30 mL
1	large purple onion, diced	1
1 tsp.	whole cumin seeds, toasted	5 mL
1 tsp.	pure chili powder	5 mL
2	bulbs roasted garlic, cloves removed	2
1/2 cup	chopped fresh cilantro	120 mL
	sea salt and freshly ground black pepper to taste	

Combine the lentils and water, bring to a boil and simmer for about 20 minutes, or until the lentils are barely cooked. Drain and set aside.

Stem the pasilla chili, slit it open and remove the seeds. Soak it in warm water until soft. Chop it finely.

Heat the oil in a sauté pan, add the onion and fry over medium heat until golden brown. Stir in the cumin seeds, chili powder and pasilla chili. Add the lentils and stir well. With the heat on medium, stir in the garlic cloves, cilantro, salt and pepper. If the mixture is sticking, add a few spoonfuls of water.

For the cod:

2–3	cloves garlic, minced	2–3
2 Tbsp.	olive oil	30 mL
1 tsp.	ground cumin	5 mL
1 Tbsp.	pure chili powder	15 mL
1/2 tsp.	dried oregano	2.5 mL
2 lbs.	fresh cod, halibut, sea bass or snapper	900 g

Preheat the oven to 375°F (190°C). Combine the minced garlic, olive oil, ground cumin, chili powder and oregano. Make a paste. Rub the paste evenly over the fish, coating it well. Heat a non-stick skillet over medium heat. Add the fish and cook it, turning once, until crusty and brown on both sides. Transfer the fish to the oven and bake for 10–12 minutes, until the fish is opaque all the way through.

To serve, place a heaping mound of the lentil mixture in the centre of the plate and top with a piece of fish.

Roasting Garlic

To roast garlic, preheat the oven to 350°F (175°C). Make a straight cut, about 1/4 inch (.6 cm) deep, across the stem end of the garlic bulb, exposing the cloves. Rub the bulb with olive oil and pour a little oil in the centre of a piece of foil. Place the garlic cut side down on the foil. Wrap the foil around the bulb. Roast for 1 hour. Don't be tempted to speed the process by raising the oven temperature—it will often result in bitter garlic. Different types of garlic from different growing regions take varying amounts of time, but it generally takes at least an hour for the sugar in the garlic to develop, giving it the characteristic mellow flavour. When it's done, it should be caramel-coloured and soft in texture. If not, return it to the oven for another 15 minutes. Let the garlic cool in the foil. Remove the cloves with a knife tip or squeeze them out of the papery husks.

—"The Girls"

Make the most of roasting garlic by doing several bulbs at a time and storing them in a tightly sealed jar in the fridge or freezer. Or take it one step further: squeeze the roasted cloves into a jar, add a thin cover of oil and refrigerate or freeze. If the garlic becomes strong, add it to the chili pot or rub it on a roast before it goes into the oven. As much as the garlic, I love the empty skins, tossing them into a jar in the freezer. Nestle them around a roast or tuck them inside a chicken for a wonderful flavour and delicious gravy. Add them to pasta or potato cooking water before they finally journey to the compost.

—Glenys Morgan

Salmon with Sweet Spice Rub and Roasted Tomato Salsa

Rubs are perfect for seafood; they impart flavour instantly and, unlike acidic marinades, they don't pull the natural juices from the fish. Serve with Golden Oven Fries (page 86) or corn on the cob and grilled asparagus. Make your own rubs using spices found in curries or Middle Eastern dishes, adding yogurt or honey.

Serves 4		Glenys Morgan
1 tsp.	cumin seed	5 mL
1 tsp.	coriander seed	5 mL
1 tsp.	chili powder	5 mL
1/2 tsp.	ground cinnamon	2.5 mL
1/4 tsp.	freshly ground black pepper	1.2 mL
2 Tbsp.	dark brown sugar	30 mL
4	6-oz. (170-g) salmon fillets (with or without skin)	4
2 Tbsp.	olive oil	30 mL
	coarse sea salt and freshly ground black pepper to taste	
1/2 cup	finely diced onion	120 mL
2 Tbsp.	olive oil	30 mL
1/2 cup	sun-dried tomatoes, finely diced, oil-packed or rehydrated	120 mL
6	Roma tomatoes, cut in half lengthwise	6
1	bulb roasted garlic	1
	coarse sea salt and freshly ground black pepper to taste	
2 Tbsp.	unsalted butter or olive oil	30 mL

Preheat the oven to 350°F (175°C).

Place the cumin and coriander in a small skillet, and dry-roast them over medium-high heat until they're warm and fragrant—a few may even pop. Once roasted, grind them in a mortar and pestle or coffee grinder. Combine the toasted spices with the chili powder, cinnamon, pepper and sugar.

Prepare the salmon by rubbing all sides with 2 Tbsp. (30 mL) olive oil. Coat the top of the salmon evenly with the spice mixture; if the pieces are thick, leaving the sides uncoated for contrasting colour is a nice touch. Let the salmon rest for 30 minutes or prepare it in advance and refrigerate. Just before cooking, sprinkle it with salt and pepper.

Sauté the onion in 2 Tbsp. (30 mL) olive oil until softened. Choose a small skillet for this step—one that can hold the tomatoes in a single layer and then go to the oven. Once the onions are soft, place the sun-dried tomatoes on the onions and arrange the Roma tomatoes, cut side down, on top. Place the skillet in the oven. After about 12–15 minutes, check the tomatoes. If the skins are wrinkled you can slip them off. When the tomato skins are removed, mix all the pan ingredients together. Squeeze the roasted garlic cloves from their skins into the mixture. Season with salt and pepper. Set aside and keep warm.

Raise the oven temperature to 400°F (200°C). Heat the butter or oil, preferably in a non-stick skillet, until very hot. Sear the spice-rubbed side of the salmon just long enough to set the spices and create a crust. Gently turn the salmon over and transfer the pan to the oven to finish cooking. Depending on the thickness, it will be done in 4–6 minutes. It should be firm to the touch, springy, not soft but definitely not hard and flaking! Serve with the warm tomato salsa.

Secret

On my first serious date after graduating from cooking school, I was planning to cook a gourmet meal to impress my date. I went shopping to find the best the local market could offer. I was thrilled to find what I thought were rather beautiful-looking tropical porgies. These small whole fish were very pretty, I thought, so I didn't want to fillet them until I could show them off. I kept them wrapped in newsprint until my dinner guest arrived, then ceremoniously unwrapped the fish to display them—much to her shock. As she told me later, she was surprised at "how big the eyeballs were and that they were going to be dinner."

—Margaret Chisholm

Salmon with Sautéed Vegetables and Balsamic Butter Sauce

I like to serve this salmon with a large mound of buttery mashed potatoes. It's a great combination and one of the staff favourites at the restaurant.

Serves 4		Deb Connors
1 cup	balsamic vinegar	240 mL
2 Tbsp.	olive oil	60 mL
4	6-oz. (170-g) salmon fillets	4
	salt and freshly ground black pepper to taste	
3 Tbsp.	unsalted butter	45 mL
1 cup	leeks, white part only, cut on the bias	240 mL
1 1/2 cups	sliced mixed mushrooms	360 mL
2 Tbsp.	white wine	30 mL
	salt and freshly ground black pepper to taste	
8 oz.	fresh spinach leaves, stems removed	225 g

In a small pan reduce the vinegar over medium-high heat until it reaches a syrupy consistency. It will reduce to approximately 2 Tbsp. (30 mL) and will take about 15 minutes. Set aside.

Preheat the oven to 450°F (230°C).

Heat the olive oil in a large sauté pan over medium heat. Season the salmon fillets with salt and pepper. When the oil is hot, place the salmon fillets in the pan, flesh side down. Sear for 1–2 minutes, depending on the thickness of the fillets. Turn the salmon skin side down, place the pan in the hot oven and cook the salmon for 4–5 minutes.

Heat the butter in a large sauté pan. When the butter is hot, add the leeks and sauté over medium-high heat until they begin to soften. Add the mushrooms and continue to sauté for 2–3 minutes. Deglaze the pan with the white wine and season with salt and pepper. Add the spinach and cook for 1 minute, or until the spinach has barely wilted. Remove from the heat.

To serve, place equal amounts of the mushroom mixture on each of 4 dinner plates. Place the cooked salmon on top of the mushrooms. Pour the butter sauce on top of the salmon and a little on the plate. To finish, drizzle a little of the balsamic reduction over the salmon and the butter sauce.

Butter Sauce

Makes about 3/4 cup (180 mL)

1 Tbsp.	butter	15 mL
2	shallots, thinly sliced	2
1 cup	dry white wine	240 mL
1 tsp.	lemon juice	5 mL
2 Tbsp.	whipping cream	30 mL
1/2 cup	diced cold butter	120 mL
	salt and white pepper to taste	

Melt the 1 Tbsp. (15 mL) butter in a small saucepan over low heat. Add the shallots and sauté gently until transparent. Add the white wine and lemon juice and cook until almost all of the liquid has evaporated. Add the cream and heat. Remove the pan from the heat, add the diced butter and whisk until smooth. Adjust the seasoning with salt and pepper. Strain. If you want the sauce a little creamier, put the finished sauce in the blender and blend on high speed for 30–60 seconds.

Chopstick Ruler

If a recipe specifies that the liquid has to be reduced to a certain amount, pour the amount of water that the liquid will be reduced to into the pot or pan that you will be using and insert a disposable chopstick. Mark the water level on the chopstick by notching it with a knife. When you are reducing the liquid and think you are close to the mark, place the chopstick into the liquid to measure it against the mark. Continue reducing and checking until the liquid is at the mark.

—Karen Barnaby

Fire-Crusted Sea Bass with Citrus Mango Relish

Inspired by the Cajun cooking of New Orleans, the seasoning mix for this fish can be used on snapper, halibut or tilapia with equal success. The relish provides a refreshing contrast to the richness of the fish and heat of the crust. Serve with basil mashed potatoes and steamed green vegetables.

Serves 6		Lesley Stowe
1 Tbsp.	paprika	15 mL
2 tsp.	salt	10 mL
1 tsp.	cayenne	5 mL
3/4 tsp.	freshly ground white pepper	4 mL
3/4 tsp.	freshly ground black pepper	4 mL
1/2 tsp.	dried thyme	2.5 mL
1/2 tsp.	dried oregano	1.5 mL
1/3 cup	melted butter	80 mL
1/3 cup	olive oil	80 mL
6	6-oz. (170-g) sea bass fillets	6
1 recipe	Citrus Mango Relish	1 recipe

Make a seasoning mix by combining the paprika, salt, cayenne, pepper, thyme and oregano. Set aside.

Preheat the oven to 375°F (190°C). Heat a large cast-iron skillet over high heat until you see white ash on the skillet bottom.

Mix the butter and olive oil in a bowl. Dip each fillet in the mixture and then generously sprinkle all sides with the seasoning mix. Place 1 or 2 fillets into the hot skillet, being careful not to overcrowd the pan, and cook uncovered until the underside looks charred, approximately 2–3 minutes. Turn over and char the other side. Set aside and repeat with the remaining fillets. When all have been charred, place all the fillets in the skillet and finish cooking in the oven, about 5–6 minutes. Serve hot with the Citrus Mango Relish spooned on the centre of each fillet.

Citrus Mango Relish

Makes 2 cups (475 mL)

1	large ripe mango, peeled, pitted and cut into 1/2-inch (2.5-cm) chunks	1
2	red grapefruit, segments separated and membranes removed	2
2	oranges, segments separated and membranes removed	2
2	limes, segments separated and membranes removed	2
2	shallots, peeled and finely diced	2
	juice of 2 lemons	
1/4 cup	extra virgin olive oil	60 mL
5	large basil leaves, finely shredded	5
	salt and freshly ground black pepper to taste	

Combine all the fruit and shallots. Stir in the lemon juice and olive oil. Add the basil just before serving and season with salt and pepper.

Citrus Segments

This makes the job of segmenting citrus fruits easier. With a sharp serrated knife (a bread knife works well), cut the top and bottom from the fruit. Place it firmly on a cutting board and with a gentle sawing motion, cut between the fruit and the white pith. Continue around the fruit until all the peel is removed. Remove any large sections of pith that you may have missed. Hold the fruit over a bowl and cut out the segments by cutting along each segment next to the membrane that is holding it in place. Remove the seeds. Use the juice in the recipe if required, or save it for drinking.

—Karen Barnaby

Porcini-Dusted Sea Bass with Balsamic Brown Butter

This fish is simply sublime. It is even more delicious if you coat it with the porcini powder the day before you serve it. This gives the flavour a chance to "bloom." You will need a coffee grinder to grind the dry mushrooms. Clean the grinder before and after using it by grinding a few spoonfuls of raw rice for 10 seconds. Serve this with Skillet-Braised Caramelized Fennel (The Girls Who Dish, page 143).

Serves 4		Margaret Chisholm
2/3 oz.	dried porcini mushrooms	20 g
4	Chilean sea bass fillets, about 6 oz. (170 g) each	4
	sea salt and freshly ground black pepper to taste	
1	tomato	1
3 Tbsp.	unsalted butter	45 mL
3 Tbsp.	red wine	45 mL
1 Tbsp.	balsamic vinegar	15 mL
1 Tbsp.	chopped chives	15 mL
	sea salt and freshly ground black pepper to taste	
	chives for garnish	

Grind the mushrooms to a very fine powder in a coffee grinder. Spread the porcini powder on a small plate. Season the sea bass generously with salt and a little pepper. Dip the sea bass in the powder, coating the fillets evenly. Place the fish on a clean plate and refrigerate for several hours or overnight.

Place enough water to cover the tomato in a pot and bring it to a boil. Cut the core out of the tomato and make a cross in the skin on the bottom. Drop the tomato into the boiling water for 20–30 seconds. Remove with a slotted spoon and place it in a bowl of ice water. When the tomato is cool, the skin will slip right off. Cut it in half horizontally. Squeeze gently to remove the seeds. Cut into 1/4-inch (.6-cm) dice.

Preheat the oven to 350°F (170°C). Heat a non-stick pan over medium heat. Add 1 Tbsp. (15 mL) of the butter and when the foam subsides, add the sea bass. Sauté for 1 minute on each side, turning the fish gently. Lift the fish out of the pan and place it on a baking sheet. Bake for 8 or 9 minutes. The fish will be a bit firm and flake slightly at the edges when done.

While the fish is cooking, add the remaining butter to the pan. Return to medium heat. Watch very carefully while the butter boils up and begins to brown. When the butter is slightly brown and smells nutty, add the red wine and balsamic vinegar and boil for 2 minutes. Add the tomato and chopped chives. Remove from the heat. Season with salt and pepper.

Spoon some sauce onto individual plates and place the sea bass on top of the sauce. Garnish with a few chives.

• • • • • •
Quick Fix:

Tuna Melties

I grew up on tuna melties. They were after-school treats prepared with my chum Christine. I first discovered my creative streak preparing tuna melties. We would open a can of tuna, squeeze the juice out for the cat and mix the tuna with lots of mayonnaise, followed by chopped pickles, celery, salt and pepper. Then we would get into mom's big spice cupboard and go nuts! You name it and it was in the mix. The tuna was then spread out on sliced bread, mounded with grated Cheddar cheese and popped in the toaster oven.

To make a more refined but still quick version, preheat the broiler. Stir together a can of drained, solid white tuna packed in water and 3 Tbsp. (45 mL) Smoked Pepper Tartar Sauce (page 129), and season with salt and pepper. Divide the tuna into 4 equal portions (so no one will fight!) and spread it on 4 slices of bread. Sprinkle each with grated cheese (I like crumbled goat cheese or freshly grated Parmesan). Place the melties on a baking sheet and broil until the cheese is melted.

—Mary Mackay

Seafood Cioppino

*Make the broth a day ahead, and assemble only fresh fish and shellfish.
You can use frozen crab legs, if necessary. If using fresh, cook the crab
early the same day, and cool, clean and refrigerate it until needed.
Serve the cioppino with lots of fresh bread or over Creamy Polenta with
Mushrooms and Leeks (page 87).*

Serves 4		Deb Connors
For the broth:		
2 Tbsp.	olive oil	30 mL
1 cup	white onion, diced	240 mL
1 cup	finely diced leek, white part only	240 mL
3 Tbsp.	chopped garlic	45 mL
4 Tbsp.	chopped parsley	60 mL
1 Tbsp.	chopped fresh thyme	15 mL
2	bay leaves	2
3 Tbsp.	tomato paste	45 mL
1/4 tsp.	hot chili flakes	1.2 mL
2 Tbsp.	chopped anchovy	30 mL
1 cup	white wine	240 mL
1 cup	tomato sauce	240 mL
2 cups	finely chopped tomatoes, seeds removed	475 mL
1 quart	clam nectar or fish stock	1 L

Heat the olive oil over medium heat in a large heavy pot. Add the onion,
leek and garlic and sauté for 4–5 minutes over medium-high heat until soft.

Reduce the heat to medium. Add the parsley, thyme, bay leaves, tomato paste,
chili flakes, anchovy and wine. Simmer until the liquid is reduced by half.

Add the tomato sauce, chopped tomatoes and stock and bring to a boil.
Reduce the heat and simmer for 5 minutes.

To assemble:

3 Tbsp.	olive oil	45 mL
1/2 lb.	mussels, scrubbed and bearded	227 g
1/2 lb.	small clams	227 g
1	Dungeness crab, cooked and cleaned, and cut into quarters	1
1/2 lb.	medium prawns, peeled and deveined	227 g
1/2 lb.	salmon, cut into chunks	227 g
1/2 lb.	halibut or other whitefish, cut into chunks	227 g
1	carrot, julienned, approximately 1/4 cup (60 mL)	1
1/2	red bell pepper, seeds and membrane removed, julienned	1/2
	salt and freshly ground black pepper to taste	

Heat the olive oil in a large shallow pan. Add the mussels, clams and crab, and sauté for 2–3 minutes over medium heat. Add the prawns, salmon and halibut, reduce the heat to low and sauté 1–2 minutes. Add the broth, carrot, red pepper, salt and pepper. Cover and simmer gently until the fish is just cooked and the clams and mussels are open.

To serve, divide the shellfish and other ingredients evenly between 4 large bowls, arranging it nicely as you go. Pour the broth over top.

Port Aperitif

Instead of wine or the ubiquitous martini, try serving your guests a glass of chilled dry white port and some warm roasted almonds before dinner.

—Lesley Stowe

Grilled Prawns with Smoked Pepper Tartar Sauce

I adore tartar sauce. I love to dip French fries in it. But tartar sauce does not always have to be served with fried foods. It is absolutely delicious with big juicy grilled prawns. The smoked pepper tartar sauce is my version of cookbook author Shirley O. Corriher's recipe. Canned chipotles in adobo sauce can be substituted for ground dried chipotle peppers. Just rinse off the sauce and use a little more as they are not as strong as the dried peppers. You can double up on the tartar sauce so there is extra to make Tuna Melties (page 125) the next day.

Serves 4		Mary Mackay
1 tsp.	finely chopped shallot	5 mL
2 tsp.	minced garlic	10 mL
1/8 tsp.	ground dried chipotle pepper	.5 mL
2 Tbsp.	olive oil	30 mL
28	large prawns, head off, tail on, deveined	28
	sea salt to taste	
1 recipe	Smoked Pepper Tartar Sauce	1 recipe

Preheat the barbecue to high.

In a large bowl stir together the shallot, garlic, chipotle and olive oil. Toss the prawns in the marinade, cover with plastic wrap and refrigerate for 30 minutes.

Thread the prawns on 4 metal skewers (if you're using bamboo skewers, presoak them in water for 30 minutes). Season with sea salt. Grill the prawns for 2–3 minutes per side. Carefully slide the prawns off the hot skewers and arrange them on plates with the sauce for dipping.

Smoked Pepper Tartar Sauce

Makes about 1/2 cup (120 mL)

1 Tbsp.	finely chopped shallot	15 mL
1/4 tsp.	ground dried chipotle pepper	1.2 mL
1 tsp.	capers, finely chopped	5 mL
2 Tbsp.	finely chopped dill pickle	30 mL
1 Tbsp.	finely chopped parsley	15 mL
1 tsp.	lemon juice	5 mL
1/2 cup	prepared mayonnaise	120 mL
1/8 tsp.	paprika	.5 mL

Place the shallot, chipotle pepper, capers, dill pickle, parsley, lemon juice, mayonnaise and paprika in the bowl of a food processor. Using the steel knife attachment, pulse the mixture for a few seconds to blend it together. It should still be slightly chunky. Refrigerate until you're ready to serve it.

Secret Craving

What is it about ranch dressing that hits a culinary chord with me? There is something about the basic tastiness of buttermilk, mayonnaise and onion, but I'm sure there is a deeper sentimental value operating here. I like to mix Dungeness crabmeat with bottled ranch dressing and a bit of red chili paste and serve it on crackers.

—Margaret Chisholm

Roasted Vegetable Chili

In an era of constant dietary changes, it becomes necessary to create really tasty recipes that fill all needs. My version of good old-fashioned chili fulfills that craving without the beef, making the meatless meal one of choice, not necessity.

Serves 6 to 8		Caren McSherry-Valagao
1	zucchini, quartered and sliced	1
2	Japanese eggplants, sliced	2
1	red bell pepper, cut into large dice	1
1	green bell pepper, cut into large dice	1
20	silverskin onions or small shallots, peeled	20
2	bulbs garlic, cloves separated and peeled	2
4 Tbsp.	good-quality olive oil	60 mL
20	cultivated white mushrooms	20
15	fresh asparagus spears	15
1	12-oz. (340-mL) can kernel corn	1
3 Tbsp.	good-quality olive oil	45 mL
1	large yellow cooking onion, diced	1
1–2	chipotle chilies, chopped	1–2
2 Tbsp.	ground cumin	30 mL
1 tsp.	Mexican oregano	5 mL
2 Tbsp.	good-quality chili powder	30 mL
4 cups	cooked black beans	950 mL
6 cups	plum tomatoes with juice, chopped (2 28-oz./796-mL cans)	1.5 L
2 cups	cooked spoon-size pasta, such as orecchiette or penne	475 mL
3/4 cup	chopped fresh cilantro	180 mL
	sea salt and freshly ground black pepper to taste	
2 cups	shredded Monterey Jack or mozzarella cheese	475 mL

Preheat the oven to 450°F (230°C). Place the zucchini, eggplant, red and green pepper, onions and garlic in a shallow roasting tray. Drizzle with the 4 Tbsp. (60 mL) olive oil, tossing the vegetables to evenly coat them with the oil. Roast in the oven for about 10 minutes. Add the mushrooms and asparagus, continuing to roast for a further 12–15 minutes, or until golden brown. Shake the pan occasionally as the vegetables roast.

Drain the corn, discarding the liquid, and place the kernels in a dry cast-iron pan. Dry-roast the corn until it dries and begins to brown, shaking the pan to prevent sticking. Set aside.

Heat the 3 Tbsp. (45 mL) olive oil in a large sauté pan. Add the onion and fry for about 5 minutes. Stir in the chilies, cumin, oregano and chili powder. Add the cooked beans to the pan along with the tomatoes, cooked pasta and cilantro. Add the roasted vegetables and dry-roasted corn, stirring well to combine. Cook until the mixture is heated through. Season with salt and pepper. Transfer the mixture to a large ovenproof serving dish. Sprinkle the cheese over the top of the chili and place under the broiler until golden brown.

• • • • • •

Quick Fix:

Chilled Soba Noodles with Salmon

While this looks long, it is quick to make. Kikkoman memmi is a bottled sauce base that is combined with water to make a broth. Soba noodles are made from buckwheat flour. As a general rule, the more expensive the soba, the better it is. The pickled ginger I use is in short julienne strips and a dark pink. It is saltier and crunchier than the sweet pickled ginger used with sushi.

Everything in this dish is available at Japanese and well-stocked Asian grocery stores. To make enough for two, start by mixing 1/2 cup (120 mL) Kikkoman memmi and 2 cups (480 mL) water together.

Soba noodles require a special cooking technique to give them their desirable bouncy texture. Half-fill a large pot with cold water and bring to a boil. Drop half a package of soba noodles into the water, a few at a time, in a continuous stream. When the water returns to a boil, add a cup (240 mL) of cold water. When it comes to a boil again, add another cup (240 mL) of cold water. Continue as above, checking the noodles frequently. When they are tender but firm, drain and rinse them under cold water. Place in two large bowls.

While the noodles are cooking, turn on the broiler and sprinkle 2 salmon fillets liberally with salt. Place the salmon skin side up on a pan and broil close to the heat. I like salmon medium-rare, cooked on one side only. If you do not share my sentiment, turn the fish over and cook it through.

Place the salmon on top of the noodles. Pour the memmi broth around the noodles. Place julienned English cucumber and a little pickled ginger on top of the salmon. Sprinkle sliced green onions and toasted sesame seeds over everything. Serve with wasabi on the side, to stir into the broth as desired.

—Karen Barnaby

Pizzas Vertes

Mama said I should eat my greens. She never said they could not come on pizza! Verte is the French word for green. These individual pizzas are topped with Pumpkin Seed Pesto, mixed greens, asparagus, zucchini and Parmesan cheese. The crusts are thin and crisp.

Makes 4 individual oval pizzas		Mary Mackay
1 1/2 cups	lukewarm water	360 mL
1/4 cup	olive oil	60 mL
3 1/4 cups	all-purpose flour	780 mL
2 Tbsp.	wheat germ	30 mL
1/2 tsp.	dry instant yeast	2.5 mL
1 1/2 tsp.	sea salt	7.5 mL
1 recipe	Pumpkin Seed Pesto	1 recipe
4	handfuls mixed salad greens	4
1/2 lb.	asparagus, cut into 1-inch (2.5-cm) pieces	227 g
1	medium zucchini, thinly sliced	1
1/4 cup	pumpkin seeds, toasted	60 mL
3/4 cup	grated Parmesan cheese	180 mL
	freshly cracked black pepper to taste	

In the bowl of a heavy-duty mixer, combine the water and olive oil. In a separate bowl, measure heaping spoonfuls of flour into measuring cups and level off for a total of 3 1/4 cups (780 mL) flour. Do not scoop the flour directly out of the bag or you will get a different amount. Stir in the wheat germ, yeast and sea salt. Add the flour mix to the bowl of the mixer. Attach a dough hook and mix on low speed for 3 minutes. Scrape down the sides of the bowl. Increase the speed to medium and mix for another 5 minutes. The dough should be moist and sticky.

Place the dough in a large greased bowl and cover with plastic wrap. Let rise in a warm, draft-free place until doubled in bulk, about 3 hours.

Lightly sprinkle the countertop with flour and turn the dough onto it. Divide the dough into 4 equal round portions. Cover with plastic wrap and let rest for 15 minutes. Roll each piece into a 1/8-inch-thick (.3-cm) oval. Place each piece on non-stick baking paper.

Preheat a pizza stone or baking sheet on the lowest shelf of a 500°F (260°C) oven.

Thin the Pumpkin Seed Pesto with a little water and brush it on the pizza dough, leaving a 1/2-inch (1.2-cm) space around the outer edge. Divide the mixed greens, asparagus and zucchini roughly into 4 portions and press them into the dough. Sprinkle on the pumpkin seeds, Parmesan cheese and black pepper.

Place 1 pizza on the pizza stone at a time. Bake until golden brown on the edges and bottom, about 12–14 minutes. Remove from the oven and drizzle with olive oil to taste. Cut the pizzas in quarters and serve immediately.

Pumpkin Seed Pesto

Makes about 1/2 cup (120 mL)

1	clove garlic	1
1/4 cup	toasted pumpkin seeds	60 mL
1/2 cup	chopped fresh basil leaves	120 mL
1 Tbsp.	chopped parsley	15 mL
1/4 cup	grated Parmesan cheese	60 mL
1/4 cup	olive oil	60 mL
1/2 tsp.	lemon juice	2.5 mL
2 Tbsp.	water	30 mL
	sea salt and freshly cracked black pepper to taste	

Place the garlic, pumpkin seeds, basil, parsley and Parmesan cheese in the bowl of a food processor. Use the steel knife attachment to blend the ingredients together. Add the olive oil, lemon juice, and water and purée until smooth. Season with salt and pepper.

Secret Craving

A totally loaded pizza. The only forgiving grace is that I always make my own dough, and then go crazy. The finishing touch is always piri piri sauce and I never forget the wine!

—Caren McSherry-Valagao

Porcini Gnocchi

*Gnocchi is one of those homey, comfort-type foods that leaves you
completely satisfied. My version incorporates dry porcini powder. If you
are lucky enough to find it already ground, buy it, it will save you
time—the time you need to sit down and enjoy another helping.*

Serves 6		Caren McSherry-Valagao
1 cup	dried porcini mushrooms	240 mL
4	large red-skinned potatoes	4
1 cup	unbleached all-purpose flour	240 mL
1	large egg, well beaten	1
	pinch of freshly grated nutmeg	
2 Tbsp.	unsalted butter	30 mL
1/2 tsp.	sea salt	2.5 mL
	freshly ground black pepper to taste	
1/3 cup	good-quality olive oil	80 mL
3	large shallots, diced	3
2	cloves garlic, minced	3
8	fresh shiitake mushrooms, sliced	8
8	brown cultivated mushrooms, sliced	8
1	portobello mushroom, sliced	1
1 cup	beef stock	240 mL
1/2 cup	heavy cream	120 mL
1/3 cup	sweet Madeira or Marsala	80 mL
	sea salt and freshly ground black pepper to taste	
	freshly grated Parmesan cheese	

Place the dried mushrooms in the bowl of a food processor and blend until
the mushrooms are almost a powder. Set aside.

Peel the potatoes and boil until tender, about 25 minutes. Drain the potatoes
and return them to the pot. Over medium-low heat, let them dry out for
about 1 minute.

When the potatoes are cool enough to handle, grate them into a large bowl.
Add the porcini powder, flour, egg, nutmeg, butter, salt and pepper. Mix well
to incorporate all the ingredients.

Turn the mixture out onto a floured board and roll it into logs about the
diameter of your thumb. Cut into 1-inch (2.5-cm) pieces and press lightly
with the tines of a fork to create a lined pattern on the gnocchi.

Bring a large pot of water to a boil. Drop the gnocchi into the water, about 10 at a time, taking care not to overcrowd them. When they rise to the surface, scoop them out with a slotted spoon and place in a buttered serving dish that's large enough to accommodate the gnocchi and the sauce.

To make the sauce, heat the olive oil in a large sauté pan; add the shallots and garlic and cook until soft but not browned. Add the mushrooms and brown lightly. Pour in the beef stock and let the sauce simmer for about 5 minutes to develop the flavour and heat it through.

Add the cream and Madeira and season with salt and pepper. Pour the hot sauce over the gnocchi and finish with plenty of Parmesan cheese.

Frozen Identities

Always clearly label what you put into the freezer. We all assume that freezing ahead gives us a night off from cooking. In reality, if what you have frozen isn't consumed within a month it never will be. A giant icecap forms over the food; you can't see or smell what is inside the container. Who would want to eat the mystery that lies beneath the ice crystals? Label it!

—Caren McSherry-Valagao

A Trio of Dry Rubs

*If I could give you one piece of advice for cooking on the barbecue
I would advise you to use dry rubs whenever possible. Wet marinades
that are full of fat and sugar can cause the barbecue to flame, which
might look dramatic, but unfortunately burns the food and deposits
awful-tasting carbon all over your dinner. These rubs have all
the seasoning built in, so with a quick dusting of rub and perhaps some
fresh garlic the food is ready to cook. Keep these rubs on hand for
an easy flavour boost to your barbecues and other dishes. They
will keep for 1 year.*

Makes 1/2 cup (120 mL) each   **Margaret Chisholm**

Ancho Chili Rub

*Avoid using supermarket chili powder for this rub. These powders are often stale
and full of cheaper chilies. It is worth seeking out high-quality ancho chili powder
from specialty shops. This rub really shows its stuff on beef; try using it on a less
expensive cut, such as flank, and cutting it into thin slices after barbecuing. Stir
a tablespoon (15 mL) into a cup (240 mL) of mayonnaise, along with a minced
clove of garlic, and you have a quick dip for grilled vegetables.*

1/4 cup	ancho chili powder	60 mL
1 Tbsp.	dry mustard	15 mL
1 Tbsp.	salt	15 mL
1 1/2 tsp.	freshly ground black pepper	7.5 mL
1 Tbsp.	sugar	15 mL
1 Tbsp.	dried thyme	15 mL

Combine everything and store in a glass jar. Sprinkle approximately 1 Tbsp.
(15 mL) dry rub per pound (454 g) of chicken, meat or vegetables.

Provençal Fish Rub

This rub gives a heady summer flavour to fish and seafood. Rub fish with a little minced garlic and good olive oil before dusting with the rub. Serve fish with ripe chopped tomatoes dressed with a little olive oil, salt and pepper for a truly Provençal experience. Prawns done in this manner are dreamy. To crush the fennel and lavender, use a mortar and pestle, pulse for a few seconds in a clean coffee grinder or crush with a rolling pin.

4 tsp.	grated orange zest	20 mL
4 Tbsp.	dried thyme	60 mL
4 tsp.	dried rosemary	20 mL
4 tsp.	crushed fennel seed	20 mL
2 tsp.	freshly ground black pepper	10 mL
4 tsp.	crushed lavender leaves (optional)	20 mL
4 tsp.	sea salt	20 mL

Dry the orange zest by spreading it on a plate for several hours or overnight. Combine all the ingredients and store in a glass jar. Sprinkle approximately 1 tsp. (5 mL) per 6 oz. (170 g) serving of fish.

Lone Star Cumin Rub

This dry rub is the most widely used spice mixture in our catering kitchen. It can be used to make fabulous chicken wings by coating the wings, spreading them loosely on a pan and roasting them at 375ºF (190ºC). Try tossing it on roasted potatoes or using it in a black bean soup. Sprinkle the finished food with chopped cilantro, which is a great "flavour pal" to this rub.

1 1/2 Tbsp.	dried thyme	22.5 mL
1 1/2 Tbsp.	sea salt	22.5 mL
2 tsp.	black pepper	10 mL
1/2 tsp.	sugar	2.5 mL
1/4 cup	ground cumin	60 mL
2 tsp.	paprika	10 mL

Combine everything and store in a glass jar. Sprinkle approximately 1 Tbsp. (15 mL) per pound (454 g) of chicken, meat, fish or vegetables.

Desserts

Gingered Apricots with Mascarpone in Pistachio Tuiles

If you are in a rush you can always skip the pistachio tuiles and serve the gingered apricots over the mascarpone in a martini glass or a champagne coupe. The tuiles can be made a few days in advance and kept in an airtight container or in the freezer. In the height of summer when fresh apricots are available, try slicing them and sautéing them in a little sugar, butter and ginger; serve them warm over the mascarpone in the tuiles.

Serves 6		Lesley Stowe
1 cup	dried apricots, cut in half	240 mL
1	2- x 1-inch (5- x 2.5-cm) strip of lemon zest	1
1/2 cup	water	120 mL
1/4 cup	sugar	60 mL
1/4 cup	chopped pistachios	60 mL
2 tsp.	sugar	10 mL
2 Tbsp.	Cointreau or orange-flavoured liqueur	30 mL
1 Tbsp.	water	15 mL
2 tsp.	finely chopped candied ginger	10 mL
2 Tbsp.	unsalted butter	30 mL
1/2 cup	mascarpone cheese	120 mL
1 recipe	Pistachio Tuiles	1 recipe

Place the apricots and lemon zest in a large saucepan, cover with the water and bring to a boil. Simmer over low heat for 5 minutes. After 5 minutes add the 1/4 cup (60 mL) of sugar, cover and continue to simmer for 5 minutes more. Remove the cover and simmer until the water has evaporated and the apricots are glossy.

Meanwhile toss the pistachios over medium heat in a dry skillet. Stir continually until they start to brown, then add the 2 tsp. (10 mL) sugar. The sugar will melt and give the pistachios a glossy look. Set aside for the garnish.

Add the liqueur, 1 Tbsp. (15 mL) water and the candied ginger to the apricots. Return to the heat and whisk in the butter. Remove from the heat. To serve, spoon some mascarpone in the bottom of a pistachio tuile, spoon the warm apricots on top and sprinkle with pistachios.

Pistachio Tuiles

Makes 6

1/4 cup	golden sugar	60 mL
1/4 cup	butter	60 mL
2 Tbsp. + 2 tsp.	corn syrup	40 mL
1/4 cup	flour	60 mL
2 Tbsp. + 2 tsp.	chopped pistachios	40 mL
	pinch salt	
1/2 tsp.	lemon juice	2.5 mL
1/4 tsp.	vanilla	1.25 mL

Melt the sugar, butter and corn syrup in a medium saucepan. Combine the flour, pistachios and salt and stir into the sugar mixture. Add the lemon juice and vanilla and stir well.

Butter 3 cookie sheets and drop 2 heaping teaspoonfuls of dough onto each sheet, making sure that each spoonful has equal room to spread out. Bake at 350°F (175°C) until the mixture bubbles and is golden, approximately 5 minutes. Remove from the oven and let cool slightly. While still warm and pliable, drape each cookie over an inverted tea cup or pudding bowl so that the cookie molds to the cup's shape. When the cookies are cool, they can be stored until needed in an airtight container.

Sticky Ingredients

When measuring sticky ingredients such as honey, molasses or corn syrup, lightly coat the inside of the cup with vegetable spray. The ingredient will slide right out.

—Deb Connors

Award-Winning Biscotti Pears with Caramel Sauce

Baked pears wrapped in a crunchy cookie crust, filled with creamy mascarpone cheese and drizzled with warm caramel sauce . . . need I say more?

Serves 4		Mary Mackay
1/4 cup	soft unsalted butter	60 mL
6 Tbsp.	sugar	90 mL
1	egg	1
1/2 tsp.	anise seed	2.5 mL
1/4 tsp.	orange zest	1.2 mL
1/8 tsp.	vanilla extract	.5 mL
1 1/4 cups	all-purpose flour	300 mL
1/2 tsp.	baking powder	2.5 mL
	pinch sea salt	
1/3 cup	finely chopped toasted hazelnuts	80 mL
4	firm pears with long stems	4
1/2 cup	mascarpone cheese	120 mL
1 recipe	Caramel Sauce	1 recipe

In a medium bowl, beat together the butter and 5 Tbsp. (75 mL) of the sugar. Add the egg, anise seed, orange zest and vanilla extract. In a separate bowl, stir together the flour, baking powder, salt and hazelnuts. Add it to the creamed butter and mix to form a dough. Divide the dough into 4 equal portions, wrap it in plastic and set it aside until you're ready to use it.

Peel the pears, leaving the stems intact. Use a melon baller to scoop the cores out of the pears and slice about 1/8-inch (.3-cm) off the bottoms so they will stand up. Use a paper towel to pat the outside of the pears dry.

Preheat the oven to 325°F (165°C). Line a baking sheet with non-stick baking paper.

On a lightly floured surface, roll each portion of biscotti dough into 1/8-inch (.3-cm) disks. Use the tip of a paring knife to poke a small hole in the centre of each disk. Wrap each pear with a disk of dough, allowing the stem to poke through the hole in the middle. Mold the dough around the pears and pinch the dough around the base of the stem to secure it. Patch up any holes or tears as you go. Do not fill the inside of the pear; leave the core opening bare.

Stand the pears up on the baking sheet. Mist the outsides of the pears with water, using a spray bottle. Sprinkle with the remaining 1 Tbsp. (15 mL) sugar. Bake the pears until golden brown, about 50 minutes. Transfer to a cooling rack.

Using a plain-tipped nozzle, fill a pastry bag with the mascarpone cheese and pipe the cheese inside the cooled pears. To serve, place the biscotti pears on plates and drizzle them with warm caramel sauce.

Caramel Sauce

Makes about 1/4 cup (60 mL)

1/4 cup	water	60 mL
1/4 cup	sugar	60 mL
3 Tbsp.	heavy cream	45 mL
1 1/2 tsp.	unsalted butter	7.5 mL

Stir the water and sugar together in a medium-sized heavy saucepan. Cover and bring to a boil over medium-high heat. Remove the lid and cook, without stirring, stirring the mixture occasionally until it starts to turn a light golden amber colour. This will take about 8 minutes. Remove from the heat. Place a sieve over the pot and pour the cream through the sieve, standing well back. The sieve will prevent splattering. When the sputtering subsides, whisk in the butter. Let the caramel sauce cool slightly before drizzling it on the pears.

Melon Baller

Using a melon baller to remove apple and pear cores was one of the most memorable tricks I learned while at cooking school. Cut your apple in half, then hold the melon baller firmly over the core and twist to scoop out the core. It is quick and clean. Make sure you buy a melon baller with a sharp edge.

—Margaret Chisholm

Sabayon of Beaumes de Venise with Armagnac Winter Fruit

This is one of my all-time favourite desserts for winter—rich, comforting and sexy. What else could one hope for in a dessert? Consider this recipe to be a blueprint—use champagne or Marsala instead of Beaumes de Venise, poached pears instead of dried fruit, and in the summer, fresh berries—raspberries, strawberries, blueberries. Beaumes de Venise is a sweet, fragrant dessert wine made from muscat grapes.

Serves 8 to 10		*Lesley Stowe*
11	egg yolks	11
1/2 cup	granulated sugar	120 mL
	pinch salt	
3/4 cup	Beaumes de Venise	180 mL
1 cup	heavy cream, whipped	240 mL
1 recipe	Armagnac Winter Fruit	1 recipe

Beat the egg yolks, sugar, salt and Beaumes de Venise together in the top of a double boiler, whisking constantly until the mixture is all one colour, about 5–10 minutes.

Remove from the heat, place the top of the double boiler in a larger bowl of ice and water and continue whisking until cool. Fold in the cream.

Place the Armagnac Winter Fruit in one large gratin dish or individual ramekins. Spoon the sabayon mixture over the fruit. Place under the broiler for 1 minute, until the surface browns slightly. Serve immediately.

Armagnac Winter Fruit

Makes 2 cups (475 mL)

1/2 cup	Armagnac	120 mL
1/2 cup	water	120 mL
1/4 cup	brown sugar	60 mL
1/2 cup	dried apricots	120 mL
1/2 cup	dried Calimyrna figs, stems removed and halved horizontally	120 mL
1/2 cup	prunes	120 mL
1	cinnamon stick	1
1	1-inch (2.5-cm) piece orange peel	1
1	1-inch (2.5-cm) piece lemon peel	1

In a heavy saucepan combine the Armagnac, water and sugar. Heat to dissolve the sugar. Add all the dried fruit, cinnamon and peel. Poach the fruit for 20 minutes or until it is soft.

Saving Vanilla Beans

Crème Anglaise is a favourite of mine and I like to use huge Tahitian vanilla beans whenever I make the sauce. Depending on the freshness and the size of the bean, you can usually use it twice. Just rinse it well with water to remove all the milk solids and dry it on the counter. When the bean is fairly dry, put it into your sugar jar. The infusion of the vanilla essence with the sugar adds something extra to whatever you use your sugar for.

—Caren McSherry-Valagao

Ricotta Puddings with Pears and Burnt Orange Sauce

When I came up with this dessert I was trying to create a simple dish reminiscent of the cooking of Sicily. It is easy to make and not too sweet. Make the chocolate shavings with a vegetable peeler or omit the chocolate and serve it with Double Chocolate and Ginger Biscotti (The Girls Who Dish, *page 184).*

Serves 8		Margaret Chisholm
3	pears	3
3 Tbsp.	butter	45 mL
6 Tbsp.	sugar	90 mL
2 cups	ricotta cheese	475 mL
2	eggs	2
2 Tbsp.	grated orange zest	60 mL
2/3 cup	sugar	160 mL
2 Tbsp.	flour	30 mL
	icing sugar	
1 recipe	Burnt Orange Sauce	1 recipe
	semi-sweet chocolate shavings	

Preheat the oven to 350º (175ºC). Butter 8 paper muffin cups and place in muffin tins, or butter 8 small ramekins.

Peel and core the pears and slice them into 1/2-inch-thick (1.2-cm) slices. Place half the butter in a large non-stick pan and melt it over medium-high heat. When the butter foams, add half the pear slices. Toss the pears in the hot butter and sprinkle on 3 Tbsp. (45 mL) of the sugar. Continue shaking the pan and tossing the pears until they are a deep caramel colour. Remove from the heat, transfer the pears to a plate and repeat with the remaining pears.

Combine the ricotta cheese, eggs, orange zest and the 2/3 cup (160 mL) sugar in a food processor. Process for about 30 seconds, until it's smooth. Transfer the mixture to a bowl. Sprinkle the flour onto the mixture and fold it in with a rubber spatula. Spoon the mixture into the muffin cups. Bake for 9 or 10 minutes, until it's lightly puffed, but not beginning to brown.

To serve, dust the puddings with icing sugar. Place 2 Tbsp. (30 mL) of the Burnt Orange Sauce on each plate, and arrange a few slices of pear and a warm pudding on top of the sauce. Garnish with chocolate shavings.

Burnt Orange Sauce

This sauce is wonderful with any chocolate pudding, cake or terrine. Make sure to allow the sugar to become a deep amber caramel before adding the orange juice; this will give it depth of flavour and make it less sweet.

Makes 1 cup (240 mL)

1 cup	sugar	240 mL
1/4 cup	water	60 mL
1 cup	orange juice	240 mL
1 Tbsp.	grated orange zest	15 mL

Place the sugar in a medium-size heavy saucepan. Add the water. Bring to a boil over high heat. Watch very carefully as the sugar begins to turn brown. Do not stir it, but give the pot a very gentle swirl. When the caramel is a deep amber, remove it from the heat. Place a sieve over the pot and pour the orange juice through the sieve, standing well back. The sieve prevents it from splattering. When it stops sputtering, return it to the heat. Add the orange zest, and boil the sauce for 1 minute. Transfer to a bowl and chill.

Chopstick Stirstick

When I melt chocolate in a microwave, I put a disposable chopstick in the bowl and leave it there while the chocolate is microwaving. When I remove the chocolate to check its progress, I use the chopstick to stir it. This eliminates messy, chocolate-coated spoons and the plates that they rest on.

—Karen Barnaby

Brandied Plum Pudding with Brandy Butter Sauce

*Plum pudding is a mainstay of Christmas holidays, but with
everything we enjoy being scrutinized for nutrition, fat and health
content, it needed an update. The old-fashioned version had fruits we
recognized, but something happened to their colour—the pineapple
turned bright red and the cherries vivid green. I have disposed of the
fake fruit and the suet and in its stead offer a plum pudding that
fits a modern lifestyle.*

Serves 8 to 10		**Caren McSherry-Valagao**
1/2 cup	currants	120 mL
1/2 cup	chopped dates	120 mL
1/4 cup	sun-dried cranberries	60 mL
1/4 cup	sun-dried cherries	60 mL
1/4 cup	sun-dried blueberries	60 mL
4	Black Mission figs, chopped	4
1/2 cup	sliced blanched almonds	120 mL
1/2 tsp.	grated lemon rind	2.5 mL
1 cup	brandy or rum	240 mL
2/3 cup	unbleached flour	160 mL
1/2 tsp.	grated nutmeg	2.5 mL
1/2 tsp.	ground cinnamon	2.5 mL
1/4 tsp.	ground ginger	1.2 mL
1/4 tsp.	ground cloves	1.2 mL
2 cups	soft bread crumbs	475 mL
1/2 cup	cold unsalted butter, grated	120 mL
3	large eggs	3
3/4 cup	sugar	180 mL

In a large bowl combine the fruit, almonds, lemon rind and 1/2 cup
(120 mL) of the brandy or rum. Stir to combine and let the mixture marinate
overnight.

The next day mix the flour and spices together. Add the bread crumbs and
then the grated butter. (To make grating the butter easier, put it in the freezer
for 1/2 hour prior to grating. Put a plastic bag over your hand so you won't
lose your grip on the butter.) Add the bread crumb mixture to the fruit

mixture, tossing with your hands to evenly mix the ingredients. In a separate bowl beat the eggs. Slowly add the sugar, beating the entire time. Pour the egg mixture over the fruit and combine it with your hands.

Butter and flour a 1 1/2-quart (1.5-L) pudding mold. Fill the prepared mold with the mixture, pushing down to make sure there are no air pockets. Butter a piece of parchment paper and place it directly on top of the mixture. Attach the lid. Place the pudding mold in a deep lidded pot and pour in enough water to come halfway up the sides of the mold. Bring the water to a boil, cover and reduce it to a simmer. Let the pudding simmer for 5 hours, adding more boiling water as you need to return it to the original level.

Remove the pudding from the water. When it's cool, remove it from the mold and wrap it in cheesecloth. Line the pudding mold with plastic wrap and place the pudding back in the mold. Pour the remaining brandy or rum over it, cover with plastic wrap and store in a cool place. The pudding should be made at least 2 weeks before serving. Check the pudding occasionally and if it seems to be drying out, add additional brandy or rum.

To serve, resteam the pudding for about 40 minutes and serve it with warm Brandy Butter Sauce.

Brandy Butter Sauce

Makes 1 1/2 cups (360 mL)

1 cup	brown sugar	240 mL
1 cup	light cream	240 mL
1/4 cup	unsalted butter	60 mL
1/4 cup	brandy	60 mL

Combine the brown sugar and light cream in a small saucepan. Cook and stir over medium heat until the sugar dissolves. Add the butter and brandy, stirring until the butter melts.

Salt Spring Island Cheese Tart with Berries

When David Wood visited the school for a class featuring his superb goat and sheep cheeses, it was my pleasure to do the cooking, demonstrating the personality of each cheese. This tart is really a tangy cheesecake, perhaps not a sweet tooth's delight. Frozen berries warmed into a compote work nicely if you can't get fresh berries.

Makes one 10-inch (25-cm) tart		Glenys Morgan
1 1/4 cups	flour	300 mL
	pinch salt	
1/4 cup	sugar	60 mL
1/2 cup	chilled unsalted butter	120 mL
3 Tbsp.	ice water	45 mL
1	egg yolk	1
6 oz.	mascarpone or cream cheese	170 g
6 oz.	unaged chèvre, available in small logs	170 g
1/2 cup	sugar	120 mL
2	eggs	2
2 cups	fresh raspberries, strawberries, blueberries, or a mixture	475 mL

Combine the flour, salt and sugar. Cut in the butter until the mixture resembles coarse oatmeal. Add the water slowly, using enough to bind the dough. Shape into a ball and flatten into a disk. Wrap in plastic wrap and chill for 1 hour before rolling.

Preheat the oven to 400°F (200°C).

Roll out the dough and fit it into a 10-inch (25-cm) tart pan with a removable bottom. Pierce the crust evenly with a fork. Line the crust with parchment and fill with baking beans or pie weights. Bake for about 10 minutes before removing the liner and weights. Bake another 10 minutes, or until the crust appears set.

Beat the egg yolk, cheeses, sugar and eggs by hand or with a mixer until the mixture is smooth. Spread it into the crust and bake until set, approximately 25 minutes. Cool before slicing. Garnish with the berries.

Chocolate Ricotta Fritters with Red Wine Cinnamon Sauce

What tasty morsels these be . . . Prep time here is a snap; it is the cooking that takes the time. They're a bit finicky but your guests will love you. Remember to watch your oil temperature because the fritters can brown outside before the inside is cooked. The key is a little batter and lots of chocolate.

Serves 8 to 10		Lesley Stowe
1 lb.	ricotta cheese	454 g
4	eggs, separated	4
1 cup	flour	240 mL
1 Tbsp.	baking powder	15 mL
2	pinches salt	2
2 tsp.	sugar	10 mL
	oil for deep frying	
1/4 lb.	Valrhona chocolate cut into 1/2-inch (1.2-cm) chunks	113 g
	icing sugar for dusting	
1 recipe	Red Wine Cinnamon Sauce (page 152)	1 recipe

Whisk the cheese and egg yolks together in a bowl. Sift the flour with the baking powder and one pinch of salt. Beat the egg whites with the other pinch of salt until soft peaks form. Beat in the sugar. Gently fold the flour mixture into the cheese mixture, then gently fold in the egg whites.

Heat 3 inches (7.5 cm) of oil in a pot to 350°F (175°C). Place a chunk of chocolate into the centre of a rounded teaspoon of batter, then carefully drop the batter into the hot oil and fry for about 2 1/2 minutes per side, until golden brown. Drain on paper towels, transfer to a serving platter, and dust liberally with icing sugar. Serve with the warm sauce.

Red Wine Cinnamon Sauce

4 cups	red wine	950 mL
2 cups	sugar	475 mL
1	cinnamon stick	1
1	2-inch (5-cm) strip of orange peel	1
2	star anise, whole	2

In a heavy saucepan combine all the ingredients. Bring to a boil and simmer to reduce until the liquid thickens enough to coat the back of a spoon, about 45 minutes.

Candied Chestnut Semifreddo with Chocolate Sauce

This semifreddo is like frozen crème brûlée—sinfully delicious. Only your imagination will limit what you can create. Substitute dried fruit or chocolate for the chestnuts and currants, or flavour it with espresso, lemon, Grand Marnier, rum, praline. . . . Although common in France and Italy, candied chestnuts are only found in specialty food stores here.

Serves 10 to 12		*Lesley Stowe*
1 cup	currants	240 mL
1/2 cup	Scotch	120 mL
8	eggs, separated	8
1 cup	sugar	240 mL
	pinch salt	
2 cups	heavy cream	475 mL
1/2 cup	candied chestnuts, roughly chopped	120 mL
1 recipe	Chocolate Sauce	1 recipe

Cover the currants with the Scotch and set aside to plump for 1 hour. Drain.

Line an 8-cup (2-L) loaf pan with parchment paper or plastic wrap. Beat the egg yolks, half the sugar and salt in a heavy pot or the top of a double boiler until thick and glossy. Set aside.

Beat the egg whites until soft peaks form. Add the remaining sugar, beating until just incorporated. Set aside.

Beat the cream to soft peaks. Fold the yolk mixture into the cream. Fold in the drained currants and the chestnuts, then fold in the egg whites. Pour the mixture into the loaf pan and freeze until firm, 6 hours or overnight. Loosen the semifreddo with a knife and unmold it. Slice it with a hot wet knife. To serve, drizzle each plate with chocolate sauce and top with a slice of semifreddo.

Chocolate Sauce

Makes 1 cup (240 mL)

8 oz.	70% bittersweet chocolate	227 g
2/3 cup	coffee	160 mL
3 Tbsp.	sugar	45 mL

Finely chop the chocolate and place it in a small heavy saucepan with the coffee and sugar. Melt the chocolate over low heat, stirring constantly.

Secret Cravings

- Most of my indulgences migrate towards chocolate. Favourites are 70% Valrhona and Scharfen Berg.
- Terra's pumpkin-seed bread toasted with crunchy peanut butter and blood orange marmalade.
- Puddings—rice, chocolate, bread! But they have to be creamy—none of that dry stodgy stuff.

—Lesley Stowe

Raspberry White Chocolate Cheesecake

This is a no-bake cheesecake which also freezes very well. Serve it with fresh raspberries in the summertime or a little purée made with frozen berries in the fall and winter. The purée makes 1 1/2 cups (360 mL). You will use 1/2 cup (60 mL) in the cake; serve the extra sauce with the cake.

Serves 12 to 16		Deb Connors

For the crust:

1 1/4 cups	graham crumbs	300 mL
1/4 cup	sugar	60 mL
1/3 cup	butter, melted	80 mL

Preheat the oven to 350°F (175°C).

Combine the graham crumbs and sugar. Add the butter and mix well. Press the crumb mixture into the bottom of a springform pan. Bake for 20 minutes, remove from the oven and let cool to room temperature.

For the raspberry purée:

2 cups	raspberries	475 mL
3 Tbsp.	sugar	45 mL
1 tsp.	cornstarch	5 mL
1 tsp.	cold water	5 mL

Purée the berries in a food processor, and strain through a fine sieve to eliminate the seeds. In a small saucepan over medium heat, bring the berry purée and sugar to a simmer and cook for 10 minutes.

Combine the cornstarch and water in a small bowl. Using a whisk, add the cornstarch to the berry purée. Simmer for 3–4 minutes, remove from the heat and let cool.

For the cheesecake mixture:

3 Tbsp.	sugar	45 mL
3 Tbsp.	warm water	45 mL
2 Tbsp.	gelatin	30 mL
2 1/2 cups	grated white chocolate	600 mL
3 Tbsp.	butter	45 mL
2 Tbsp.	water	30 mL
3 cups	softened cream cheese	720 mL
1 1/3 cups	sour cream	320 mL
3	large eggs	3
1/2 tsp.	vanilla	2.5 mL

Combine the sugar and warm water in a small bowl. Sprinkle the gelatin over the top, and stir until the gelatin dissolves.

Place a metal bowl over a pot of hot water, making sure the water does not touch the bottom of the bowl. Combine the grated chocolate, butter and water in the bowl. Turn the heat to low and stir frequently. As the chocolate melts, whisk until smooth.

Place the cream cheese in the bowl of an electric mixer and process at medium speed until fluffy. Mix in the sour cream. Add the eggs one at a time, beating well after each addition. Add the vanilla, turn to low speed, and add the melted white chocolate and the gelatin mixture.

To assemble:
Spread 1/2 of the cheese mixture on the bottom of the springform pan. Drizzle with 1/4 cup (60 mL) of the berry purée. Top with the rest of the cheesecake mixture followed by 1/4 cup (60 mL) of the purée. Pull a wooden skewer through the last layer of purée to create a design.

Lightly cover the cake with plastic wrap and refrigerate overnight. This cheesecake also freezes very well. Freeze it in the springform pan overnight. Remove it from the pan and double wrap with plastic wrap. Place it back in the freezer and it will keep well for up to 2 weeks. When you want to defrost it, remember to take off the plastic wrap while the cake is still frozen. Place the cake on a serving plate and let it defrost in the refrigerator. This will take about 5 or 6 hours.

Stu's Mascarpone "Cheesecake" with Plum Compote

Thank you Stu! Glorious, and gloriously easy to make. Advise your guests to attack the cheesecake from the middle, not from the sides. Go seasonal and use fresh berries instead of the plum compote if you prefer.

Makes 8 servings		Karen Barnaby
1/2 lb.	cream cheese at room temperature	227 g
1/2 cup	granulated sugar	120 mL
1 tsp.	vanilla extract	5 mL
12 oz.	mascarpone cheese, at room temperature	340 g
2 cups	whipping cream, chilled	480 mL
6	sheets phyllo pastry	6
3/4 cup	melted butter	180 mL
6 Tbsp.	brown sugar	90 mL
1 recipe	Plum Compote	1 recipe

Either by hand with a whisk or with an electric mixer, beat the cream cheese, sugar and vanilla together on high until it's light and fluffy, scraping down the bowl occasionally. Add the mascarpone and beat only until incorporated. Whip the cream to soft but firm peaks and fold it into the cheese mixture. The cheese mixture can be made up to a day in advance. Cover and refrigerate.

Preheat the oven to 400°F (200°F).

Lay a sheet of phyllo out on your work surface and brush with butter. Sprinkle evenly with 1 1/2 Tbsp. (22.5 mL) sugar. Place a second sheet over the first and press firmly over the entire surface. Brush with butter and sprinkle evenly with another 1 1/2 Tbsp. (22.5 mL) sugar. Cover with a third sheet of phyllo and press firmly again. Brush generously with butter. Cut the sheet in thirds lengthwise and in quarters widthwise to make 12 even squares. Carefully transfer to a baking sheet lined with parchment paper. Repeat the above procedure with the remaining phyllo, butter and sugar.

Bake one tray at a time for 4–4 1/2 minutes until very lightly browned. Transfer to a wire rack to cool. The squares may be made a day in advance and kept in a tightly covered container.

Just before serving, assemble the cheesecakes. Place a square of phyllo in the middle of a plate. Place a large dollop of the mascarpone mixture in the middle of the square. Top with a phyllo square and another large dollop of the mascarpone mixture. Cover with the third square. Spoon the plum compote over the top and serve immediately.

Plum Compote

Makes 2 cups (475 mL)

12	plums, peeled, pitted and quartered	12
1/4 cup	water	60 mL
1/3 cup	granulated sugar	80 mL
1/2	cinnamon stick	1/2
	pinch turmeric	

Place all the ingredients in a heavy pot and cook over high heat until the plums begin to fall apart. Remove from the heat and transfer to a bowl to cool. The plums may be made 3 days in advance. Cover and refrigerate.

Apple Tart

This tart is actually easy to make—you can do it in stages over a day or two if you wish. The pastry recipe makes enough dough for 2 tarts, so you can freeze the remainder for another day.

Serves 8 to 12		Deb Connors
For the crust:		
1/2 cup	butter, at room temperature	120 mL
2/3 cup	sugar	160 mL
2	eggs	2
2 cups	pastry flour	475 mL
1	egg white, beaten	1

Cream the butter, add the sugar and beat until it is incorporated. Add the eggs one at a time, scraping down the bowl and beating after each addition. Add the flour all at once and mix until just blended. Divide the dough into 2 equal pieces. Wrap them in plastic wrap and freeze for 2 hours.

Turn one piece of dough onto a lightly floured surface and while it is still frozen, roll it into a 14-inch (36-cm) circle, about 1/8 inch (.3 cm) thick. Fit it into a 12-inch (30-cm) tart pan with a removable bottom. Roll over the top of the tart pan with your rolling pin to cut the excess dough away from the pan. Place the crust in the freezer for 30 minutes.

Preheat the oven to 350°F (175°C). Fit a piece of foil into the tart shell, fill it with pie weights or dried legumes, and blind bake for 5 minutes. Remove from the oven, take out the weights and brush the tart shell with egg white. Return the tart shell to the oven and bake for 2 minutes more. Cool.

For the frangipane:		
1/2 cup + 1 Tbsp.	butter	135 mL
3/4 cup	sugar	180 mL
4	egg yolks	4
1 Tbsp.	Calvados	15 mL
2 Tbsp.	cream	30 mL
1 1/2 cups	ground almonds	360 mL

Cream the butter and sugar together. Add the yolks one at a time, beating well after each addition. Using a whisk, slowly add the Calvados and cream. Fold in the almonds.

To assemble the tart:

5	large apples, peeled, cored and sliced 1/8 to 1/4 inch (.3 to .6 cm) thick	5
2 Tbsp.	unsalted butter, melted	30 mL
1 Tbsp.	sugar	15 mL

Preheat the oven to 325°F (165°C). Spread the frangipane in an even layer on the bottom of the baked tart shell. Fan the thinly sliced apples in a single layer over the frangipane, starting at the centre and working out toward the edge in a circular direction. Bake the tart for 10 minutes. Brush the tart with the melted butter and sprinkle with the 1 Tbsp. (15 mL) sugar. Bake for 30–35 minutes more.

• • • • • •

Quick Fix:

Poached Figs and Ice Cream

Cut 2 dried figs per person in half lengthwise and place in a large saucepan. Cover in red wine and half as much sugar. Add a cinnamon stick. Bring to a boil and simmer until the figs are soft. Raise the heat and cook until the wine reduces slightly. Serve over best-quality vanilla or chocolate ice cream.

—Lesley Stowe

Fresh West Coast Plum Tart

In my opinion desserts are the headache of dinner parties. Everyone expects you to be Lesley Stowe, the Queen of Desserts, but let's face it, by the time you clean the house, shop, prepare the appetizer, starter, salad, main course and then try to tackle the finale of the evening, perfection is not the word that comes to mind. Easy, quick and make-ahead probably are the words you're looking for. This tart is free-form, meaning that however it turns out is the way it should be. Apples are a great substitute; just remember the high heat makes the crust crispy. Pray for leftovers—I just love it for breakfast with my cappuccino.

Serves 6 to 8		Caren McSherry-Valagao
1 1/4 cups	unbleached all-purpose flour	300 mL
	pinch sea salt	
1/2 tsp.	sugar	2.5 mL
7 1/2 Tbsp.	cold unsalted butter	112.5 mL
4 Tbsp.	ice water	60 mL
1/3 cup	sugar	80 mL
1/2 cup	ground hazelnuts	120 mL
4	soda biscuits, crushed	4
1 lb.	fresh prune plums, halved and stoned	454 g
3 Tbsp.	unsalted butter	45 mL
1/4 cup	good-quality apricot jam	60 mL

For the pastry, sift the flour into a large bowl, add the salt and 1/2 tsp. (2.5 mL) sugar. Cut in the 7 1/2 Tbsp. (112.5 mL) butter with a pastry blender until the butter pieces are a little larger than peas. Add the water all at once, mixing the dough together as quickly as possible; overworking the pastry makes it tough. Wrap the dough in plastic wrap and chill for 15 minutes.

Mix the 1/3 cup (80 mL) sugar, hazelnuts and soda biscuits together. Set aside.

Preheat the oven to 400°F (200°C) degrees. Roll the dough until it is very thin, 1/8 inch (.3 cm), making a shape roughly 12 inches (30 cm) wide and 16 inches (40 cm) long. Fold it in half to make it easy to lift onto a flat baking sheet. Open the dough flat, sprinkle half of the sugar-hazelnut mixture on the bottom and evenly distribute the plums in a single layer.

Leave a 2-inch (5-cm) border around the entire tart. Sprinkle the remaining half of the sugar mixture over top and dot with the 3 Tbsp. (45 mL) butter.

Fold the border back over the plums and bake the tart for about 1 hour and 10 minutes, or until the pastry is golden brown and the plums are cooked. Heat the apricot jam until it melts and gently brush the edges of the pastry and the top of the fruit with the jam. Serve warm or at room temperature. Ice cream is a nice garnish.

Secret Craving

Whenever we have a family holiday gathering there is never any shortage of baked goods. I usually show up with treats from our bakery because I am too tired to prepare something at home over the busy holiday season. My sister Florence brings tasty low-fat baked goods. My other sister Georgina is a good baker, but she usually arrives with some fancy store-bought pastries. Of all these desserts my favourite is my mom's lemon cake, made from a mix. It is always moist and tender, even when it is several days old. The cake itself is not terribly lemony but the icing she pours on top has chopped lemon zest in it. My sisters always give me a hard time when I pass up the other baked goods for my mom's cake. They think it is quite sad that I—as a professional baker—would choose my mom's lemon cake mix over fresh baked goods.

—Mary Mackay

Rhubarb and Strawberry Crumble

Rhubarb is one of those foods that you either love or hate. My husband detests the stuff, I love it, and therein lies the challenge—trying to disguise it to see if he will uncover the truth of what he is eating. Sadly, he always does. Here is one of those trials, using strawberries as the cover-up. I know you will love it. Serve it with a good-quality ice cream.

Serves 4 to 6		Caren McSherry-Valagao
2 cups	coarsely chopped rhubarb	475 mL
1/2 cup	granulated sugar	120 mL
1	small orange, zest only	1
3 Tbsp.	orange liqueur	45 mL
1 cup	fresh strawberries, quartered	240 mL
5 Tbsp.	soft unsalted butter	75 mL
1/2 cup	rolled oats	120 mL
2/3 cup	unbleached all-purpose flour	160 mL
1 tsp.	ground cinnamon	5 mL
1/2 cup	brown sugar, lightly packed	120 mL
1/2 cup	crushed amaretti cookies	120 mL

String the rhubarb before chopping if it appears to be thick and tough. When you measure it, the cups should be heaping. Sprinkle the sugar over the rhubarb and let it sit for about 15 minutes. Preheat the oven to 350°F (175°C).

Finely chop the orange zest, and add it to the rhubarb along with the liqueur and strawberries. Place this mixture in a shallow, 3- to 4-cup (720- to 950-mL) gratin dish. Set aside.

To make the topping, combine the butter, oats, flour, cinnamon and brown sugar in a bowl. Using your hands, crumble the mixture until it forms coarse crumbs. Add the amaretti cookies.

Spread the topping evenly over the rhubarb mixture. Bake for 45 to 60 minutes. The crumble should be crisp and lightly browned. Serve warm.

Blackberry Apple Crisp

This can be made in the morning and warmed before serving, or served warm out of the oven with vanilla ice cream or whipping cream. Substitute your favourite berry for the blackberries.

Serves 4 to 6		**Deb Connors**
2 lbs.	apples, peeled, cored, and cut into 1/2-inch (1.2-cm) slices	900 g
1/3 cup	butter, cut into small cubes	80 mL
2 1/2 cups	blackberries, fresh or frozen	600 mL
1/2 cup	sugar	120 mL
1 Tbsp.	instant tapioca	15 mL
1 1/3 cups	flour	320 mL
1 1/3 cups	sugar	320 mL
1 1/2 cups	rolled oats	360 mL
1/2 cup + 1 Tbsp.	cold butter, cut into small cubes	165 mL

Preheat the oven to 350ºF (175ºC). In a medium bowl, combine the apples, 1/3 cup (80 mL) butter, blackberries, 1/2 cup (120 mL) sugar and tapioca.

To make the topping, place the flour, 1 1/3 cups (320 mL) sugar and oats in a large bowl and mix well by hand. Add the butter and work the mixture until it resembles coarse crumbs, using a pastry blender or by hand.

Lightly oil a 10- x 10-inch (25- x 25-cm) baking dish. Spread the fruit mixture into the dish. Cover with the crumb topping. Place the dish on a baking sheet and bake until the apples are cooked and the topping is browned, about 50 minutes.

Banana Chocolate Chiffon Cake with Bourbon Cream

This is a combination of two childhood memories—a moist, dense banana and sour cream cake that my mother made in a small tube pan, and the yogurt sprinkled with brown sugar my grandmother fed me. This cake is moist and marvellous on its own or can be dressed up with the Bourbon Cream. To grate chocolate, either use the grating attachment of a food processor or put a plastic bag over your hand to hold the chocolate and grate it on a box grater.

Serves 12		Karen Barnaby
1 cup	egg whites, from approximately 8 large eggs	240 mL
1/2 tsp.	cream of tartar	2.5 mL
2 1/4 cups	sifted cake flour	535 mL
1 1/4 cups	sugar	300 mL
1 Tbsp.	baking powder	15 mL
1 cup	grated bittersweet chocolate	240 mL
1/2 tsp.	salt	2.5 mL
5	large egg yolks	5
1 cup	very ripe mashed bananas	240 mL
1/2 cup	vegetable oil	120 mL
3 Tbsp.	bourbon	45 mL
3 Tbsp.	water	45 mL
1 tsp.	vanilla	5 mL

Preheat the oven to 325°F (165°C). Have an ungreased 10-inch (25-cm) tube pan at hand with a removable bottom. Do not use a non-stick pan.

In a large bowl, combine the egg whites and cream of tartar. With an electric mixer, beat on high speed to stiff but moist peaks.

Stir the flour, sugar, baking powder, chocolate and salt together. Make a well in the dry ingredients and add the egg yolks, banana, oil, bourbon, water and vanilla. With an electric mixer, beat the ingredients in the centre of the well, gradually drawing in the dry ingredients. Beat just until smooth. Pour 1/3 of the batter over the egg whites and fold it in quickly but thoroughly. Repeat twice with the remaining batter.

Pour the batter into the pan and bake on the middle rack of the oven for 55 minutes. Increase the temperature to 350°F (175°C) and bake for 10–15 minutes longer, until a cake tester inserted into the centre comes out clean. Immediately remove from the oven and turn upside down. Most tube pans have "feet" that will support the pan while upside down. If yours does not, hang the pan upside down from the centre tube over the neck of a bottle. Let cool completely.

Turn the pan right side up and run a long, thin-bladed knife around the inside and outside of the cake. Invert onto a plate and remove the outside of the pan. Run the knife between the top of the pan and the cake and remove the top of the pan. Serve with the Bourbon Cream if you like.

Bourbon Cream

Makes 1 3/4 cups (420 mL)

1 1/2 cups	sour cream	360 mL
1/4 cup	bourbon	60 mL
1/2 cup	brown sugar	120 mL

Mix the sour cream and bourbon together. Just before serving, sprinkle the brown sugar on top of the sour cream mixture and fold it in, leaving large streaks of brown sugar through the mixture for a contrast of flavour and texture.

• • • • • •

Quick Fix:

Crème Fraîche

To make quick crème fraîche, combine 1 cup (240 mL) heavy cream with 1 Tbsp. (15 mL) sour cream. Let the mixture sit overnight at room temperature, then refrigerate.

—Deb Connors

Fifteen Minutes of Fame Chocolate Torte

The most earnest people in the kitchen are those who don't cook but know they'd love to create a special treat for someone, even once. I often teach this dessert to these kind spirits. It's a classic yet easy technique and the result is a truffle-like chocolate wonder. The fame comes when it's being eaten and the fifteen minutes is the time it takes in the oven.

Serves 8 to 10		Glenys Morgan
1 tsp.	butter for preparing the pan	5 mL
1 lb.	semi-sweet chocolate, chopped into small pieces	454 g
2 Tbsp.	brewed coffee	30 mL
2/3 cup	unsalted butter at room temperature	160 mL
4	large eggs, separated	4
1 Tbsp.	flour	15 mL
1 Tbsp.	sugar	15 mL

Prepare an 8-inch (20-cm) springform or layer pan by fitting the bottom with parchment or wax paper. Butter the sides of the pan and the top of the parchment liner. Preheat the oven to 425°F (220°C).

Using a double boiler, melt the chocolate with the brewed coffee. The coffee helps the chocolate to melt without changing flavour or consistency. Remove the double boiler from the heat; stir in the 2/3 cup (160 mL) butter by spoonfuls.

In a small bowl, beat the egg yolks until light and creamy coloured. Add a small amount of the melted chocolate to the eggs. Whisk the remaining chocolate slowly into the tempered egg yolks. Add the flour to the mixture.

In a large clean bowl—preferably stainless—beat the egg whites until soft peaks form. Add the sugar. Beat until firm but not dry. Fold some of the egg whites into the chocolate to lighten the texture. Turn the chocolate into the egg whites and fold them together. (Folding is easier with a giant spatula.) Angle the bowl so the spatula can turn rather than stir the whites.

Turn the mixture into the prepared pan and bake for 15 minutes. The cake will appear underdone. Remove it from the oven and run a knife around the edge of the cake. Cool in the pan, loosen it again with a knife and turn out.

Slice into small pieces and serve with a dusting of cocoa or icing sugar and berries. The cake will have superior chocolate flavour if it's made a day ahead and chilled well.

To freeze, wrap with plastic wrap and foil to keep unwanted flavours out. A tightly wrapped cake will keep quite a long time in the freezer. Before serving, thaw it gently in the refrigerator for about 2 hours. Serve slightly chilled.

Lemon Meringue Kisses

All right, so I got this idea from a popular food magazine. It just looked too darn good to pass up. I can take credit for its cute name and my own special touches have changed the recipe. These crisp lemony meringues melt in your mouth. They look like great big white Hershey Chocolate Kisses but without all the fat!

Makes 35 kisses		Mary Mackay
2	large egg whites, about 1/4 cup (60 mL)	2
1/8 tsp.	cream of tartar	.5 mL
1/2 cup	sugar	120 mL
1/8 tsp.	cornstarch	.5 mL
3/4 tsp.	finely chopped lemon zest	4 mL
1 recipe	Lemon Curd (page 168)	1 recipe

Preheat the oven to 200°F (95°C). Line a baking sheet with non-stick baking paper.

Place the egg whites and cream of tartar in the bowl of a heavy-duty mixer. Using the whisk attachment, beat the egg whites until they form soft peaks when the whisk is lifted. Gradually beat in the sugar and cornstarch, beating just until the meringue holds stiff, glossy peaks. Fold in the lemon zest.

Transfer the meringue to a pastry bag fitted with a 1/2-inch (1.2-cm) plain-tipped nozzle. Pipe the kisses onto the baking sheet. They should be about 1 1/4 inches (3 cm) in diameter. Bake on the middle rack of the oven for 50 minutes. Turn off the oven and let the meringues sit in the oven for 1 hour. Serve the meringues with a bowl of lemon curd for dipping.

Lemon Curd

Makes about 1 cup (240 mL)

2	large egg yolks	2
1	large egg	1
1/4 cup	sugar	60 mL
4 Tbsp.	lemon juice	60 mL
1 1/2 tsp.	finely chopped lemon zest	7.5 mL
1/4 cup	unsalted butter, cut into 4 pieces	60 mL

In a medium-size metal bowl, whisk together the egg yolks and egg, sugar, lemon juice and lemon zest. Set the bowl over a saucepan of simmering water. Don't let the bottom of the bowl touch the water. Whisk in the pieces of butter. Continue whisking and cook until the mixture starts to thicken, about 4–6 minutes. Check the temperature with a candy thermometer; it should reach 160°F (70°C).

Remove the bowl from the saucepan and strain the curd into a serving dish. Cover the surface with a piece of plastic wrap. Refrigerate the lemon curd until you're ready to serve it.

• • • • • •
Quick Fix:

Ice Cream Sandwiches

This treat requires only a box of thin crisp cookies and a carton of premium ice cream.

Store the cookies in the freezer with the ice cream. This will make the preparation easier as the ice cream will not begin to melt between the cookies. Place a spoonful of ice cream between two cookies. Gently squeeze the cookies together and run the edge of a spoon around the outside edge of the sandwich to remove any ice cream that squishes out. Place the ice cream sandwich on a plate in the freezer while you prepare the rest of the sandwiches. Make as many as you can eat!

—Mary Mackay

Cardamom Apple Cake

This fabulously moist loaf cake is filled with large chunks of apple perfumed with cardamom. It is perfect with a carefully brewed pot of high-quality tea served with a wee bit of ceremony.

Makes one 10-inch (25-cm) cake		Margaret Chisholm
1 cup	unsalted butter, softened to room temperature	240 mL
1 1/3 cups	sugar	320 mL
2	eggs	2
1 tsp.	vanilla	5 mL
1/2 cup	orange juice	120 mL
2 Tbsp.	orange zest	30 mL
2 cups	all-purpose flour	480 mL
2 tsp.	ground cinnamon	10 mL
1 1/2 tsp.	ground cardamom	7.5 mL
1/2 tsp.	baking soda	2.5 mL
1 tsp.	baking powder	5 mL
1/2 tsp.	salt	2.5 mL
3	McIntosh apples	3
	icing sugar	

Preheat the oven to 350°F (175°C). Grease and flour a 10-inch (25-cm) springform pan or a 9- × 5-inch (23- × 12-cm) loaf pan.

Beat the butter and sugar until pale and light. Add the eggs and continue beating until well combined. Stir in the vanilla, orange juice and orange zest. In a separate bowl, combine the flour, cinnamon, cardamom, baking soda, baking powder and salt.

Core the apples, but leave the peel on. Chop the apples into coarse chunks. Add the dry ingredients to the sugar mixture, folding it together until it's just mixed. Fold in the apples. Scrape the batter into the prepared pan. Bake for 1 hour or until a toothpick comes out clean when tested in the centre of the cake. Remove from the oven and allow to cool for 5 minutes. Remove the cake from the pan and cool it on a rack. Dust with icing sugar before serving.

Oatmeal Raisin Cake with Broiled Coconut Cashew Icing

I started making this cake 20 years ago, before food became a form of entertainment or cause for paranoia and was eaten just because it tasted good. This cake still tastes good.

Makes one 9-inch (23-cm) cake		Karen Barnaby
1/2 cup	all-purpose flour	120 mL
1 tsp.	baking soda	5 mL
1 tsp.	ground cinnamon	5 mL
1/2 tsp.	ground allspice	2.5 mL
1/4 tsp.	salt	1.2 mL
2 cups	large-flake rolled oats	480 mL
2/3 cup	unsalted butter, at room temperature	160 mL
1/2 cup	golden raisins	120 mL
1.1/4 cups	boiling water	300 mL
1 cup	light brown sugar	240 mL
2	eggs	2
1 cup	brown sugar	240 mL
1/2 cup	butter	120 mL
1/2 cup	whipping cream	120 mL
1 cup	roasted cashew pieces	240 mL
1 1/2 cups	unsweetened large-flake coconut	360 mL

Preheat the oven to 325°F (165°C). Butter and flour a 9-inch (23-cm) springform pan.

Sift together the flour, baking soda, cinnamon, allspice and salt. Combine the oats, 2/3 cup (160 mL) butter and raisins. Pour the boiling water over the oats. Allow to cool completely, stirring occasionally. Beat in the 1 cup (240 mL) light brown sugar and eggs, then the flour mixture. Pour the batter into the prepared pan and bake for 35–40 minutes, until a cake tester comes out clean. Place on a rack to cool.

To make the icing, combine the 1 cup (240 mL) brown sugar, 1/2 cup (120 mL) butter and whipping cream in a heavy pot. Bring to a boil and cook, stirring occasionally, for 3 minutes. Remove from the heat and stir in the cashews and coconut. Allow to cool slightly, then spread it over the top of the cake. Heat the broiler to high. Place the cake about 4 inches (10 cm) below the heat and broil until the icing is brown and bubbly. Place on a rack and allow the cake to cool completely before removing it from the pan.

Chocolate Truffles

Chocolate truffles get their name because of their uneven, irregular shape, like the savoury truffles that grow beneath oak trees in the forests of Italy and France. However, that is where the resemblance ends. These chocolate truffles possess all the wonderful qualities that make it almost impossible to stop at one. They make terrific gifts boxed and ribboned. Be the hero of every chocoholic on your list.

Makes 36 pieces		Caren McSherry-Valagao
1 cup	heavy cream	240 mL
1 1/4 lbs.	semi-sweet or white chocolate, such as Valrhona or Callebaut	565 g
2 Tbsp.	liquor of your choice, such as Grand Marnier, cognac or rum	30 mL
	your choice of coating, such as icing sugar, toasted chopped nuts (pistachios, almonds, pecans, etc.), dark Dutch-process cocoa powder or melted chocolate	

Place the cream in the top of a double boiler and bring the water to a boil. Chop the chocolate into 1/2-inch (1.2-cm) chunks. Turn off the heat, add the chocolate to the hot cream and stir until the chocolate is melted. Stir in the liquor. Pour the mixture into a shallow bowl and chill until the chocolate is firm.

Scoop small balls onto a cookie sheet lined with parchment paper. You can use a tiny ice cream scoop, available at specialty cookware stores, to scoop the truffles. If they begin to soften, chill to firm them up. Place each of the coating ingredients into separate shallow dishes. Roll the chocolate truffles in your choice of coating and keep refrigerated until serving time.

The truffles will keep for several weeks under refrigeration. Store in a tightly covered container between sheets of wax paper.

Chocolate, Cherry and Anise Bread

I have always wanted to sell a chocolate and cherry loaf at the bakery but there is another bakery in Vancouver that is also well known for its breads, especially their chocolate-cherry loaf. I am still kicking myself for not having come up with it first. In order to get over this, here is my version of a chocolate, cherry and anise bread. This yeast-risen loaf is not very sweet and lends itself well to sweet toppings.

Makes two 1-lb. (454-g) loaves		Mary Mackay
1 1/2 cups	lukewarm water	360 mL
1 3/4 tsp.	dry instant yeast	9 mL
3 1/4 cups	white bread flour	780 mL
1/3 cup	Dutch-process cocoa powder	80 mL
6 Tbsp.	honey	90 mL
1 1/2 tsp.	sea salt	7.5 mL
5 Tbsp.	unsalted butter, room temperature	75 mL
1 Tbsp.	anise seed	15 mL
4 oz.	semi-sweet chocolate chunks, or chocolate chips	113 g
1/2 cup	chopped dried cherries	60 mL
1 Tbsp.	coarse sugar or sugar crystals	15 mL

In a medium bowl, combine 1 cup (240 mL) of the water, 3/4 tsp. (4 mL) of the yeast and 1 cup (240 mL) of the flour. Measure heaping spoonfuls of the flour into a measuring cup and level off; do not scoop the flour directly out of the bag, as you will get a different amount. Stir until smooth. Cover the sponge with plastic wrap and let sit at room temperature for 8–12 hours. The sponge can then be refrigerated until you're ready to use it (up to 12 hours).

In the bowl of a heavy-duty mixer, combine the sponge, the remaining 1/2 cup (120 mL) water, the cocoa powder and honey. Whisk until the cocoa powder is blended in. Add the remaining 2 1/4 cups (535 mL) flour (filling the measuring cup as above, by the spoonful), 1 tsp. (5 mL) yeast and the salt. Attach a dough hook and mix on low speed for 3 minutes. Scrape down the sides of the bowl. Increase the speed to medium and mix for 4 minutes. Add the butter and anise seed and mix to incorporate. Mix in the chocolate and cherries on low speed. The dough should be moist and sticky.

Place the dough in a large greased bowl and cover with plastic wrap. Let it rise in a warm draft-free place for 90 minutes. Punch the dough down and turn it over in the bowl. Cover it with plastic wrap and let it rise for 1 hour.

Turn the dough out onto a lightly floured work surface and sprinkle the top with flour. Press down on the dough to release most of the trapped air bubbles. Divide the dough in half and shape it into 2 round loaves. Sprinkle an unrimmed baking sheet with flour and place the loaves on the baking sheet, leaving space between them. Lightly sprinkle the tops of the loaves with flour and loosely cover with plastic wrap. Let rise until doubled in bulk, about 90 minutes.

Preheat a pizza stone or baking sheet on the second-lowest shelf in a 450°F (230°C) oven. Place an empty rimmed baking sheet on the bottom shelf to heat.

Mist the top of the loaves with water and sprinkle with coarse sugar. Use a sharp knife to cut a 1/2-inch (1.2-cm) star pattern across the top of each loaf. Open the oven door and slide the loaves onto the baking sheet or pizza stone. Immediately pour water into the empty baking sheet to create a burst of steam, and using a spray bottle filled with water, quickly spray the inside of the oven. Avoid spraying the oven light.

Bake for 10 minutes, then lower the temperature to 375°F (190°C). Bake until the loaf sounds hollow when tapped on the bottom, another 35–40 minutes. Remove from the oven and cool on a wire rack.

Note: If time is limited the sponge can be omitted. Just add the sponge amounts into the mixer with the rest of the ingredients and proceed. The bread freezes well.

Pizza Stone

To replicate a hearth oven like the one in our bakery, I use a pizza stone and a pizza paddle in my oven at home. They can both be purchased at kitchen supply stores and I highly recommend them for any bread making. A pizza stone is a flat ceramic clay tile. Purchase a square stone rather than a round one as it gives a larger surface area on which to bake. The pizza paddle is a lightweight piece of wood designed to easily transfer loaves onto pizza stones in the oven.

—Mary Mackay

My Mother's Pre-Biscotti Biscotti

Anyone familiar with Jewish cooking will recognize these as mandelbrot. I don't know where my mother got the recipe, but they were part of her repertoire for quite a while. They seemed almost bland compared to the usual childhood cookies, but that is their appeal. I treasured the sweet, crunchy, adult flavour of these biscuits, and still do.

Makes approximately 24		*Karen Barnaby*
3 1/2 cups	flour	840 mL
2 tsp.	baking powder	10 mL
1/4 tsp.	salt	1.2 mL
3	eggs	3
1 cup	vegetable oil	240 mL
1 cup	sugar	240 mL
1 cup	walnut pieces	240 mL
1/2 cup	sugar	120 mL
2 tsp.	cinnamon	10 mL

Preheat the oven to 350°F (175°C). Line a baking sheet with parchment paper.

Sift the flour, baking powder and salt together. Beat the eggs, oil and 1 cup (240 mL) sugar together until well combined. Stir in the flour mixture and walnuts. Shape into two 12- x 3-inch (30- x 7.5-cm) logs and transfer to the baking sheet. Bake for 30 minutes. Remove to a rack to cool slightly, then transfer to a cutting board and cut into 1-inch (2.5-cm) slices with a serrated knife. Transfer, cut sides up, to baking sheets and bake for 5–8 minutes longer until dry.

Combine the 1/2 cup (120 mL) sugar with the cinnamon. Roll the cookies in this mixture while warm and transfer to racks to cool. Store in an airtight container.

Drop Cookies

When preparing drop cookies use an ice-cream scoop to measure out the dough. This will give you uniformly sized cookies and a more even bake.

—Mary Mackay

Crispy Chocolate and Black Pepper Shortbread

Think of these as cookies for the biscotti-challenged. No rolling pin required and no eggs. Thin and crispy, they're delicious with coffee or ice cream. Score and cut them into long pointy triangles and make a variety of sizes. At Christmas, small helpers can pat the dough into the pan and safely score shapes with even the biggest cutters. They must be scored while warm and cooled to a crisp texture.

Makes an 11- x 17-inch (28- x 43-cm) pan		Glenys Morgan
1 1/2 cups	dark brown sugar	360 mL
3 cups	flour	720 mL
1/2 tsp.	baking soda	2.5 mL
1/2 cup	cocoa powder	120 mL
1 tsp.	coarsely ground black pepper	5 mL
1 1/2 cups	unsalted butter	360 mL

Preheat the oven to 375°F (190°C). Mix the sugar, flour and baking soda together. Add the cocoa and pepper. Add the butter and mix into a smooth cookie dough.

Press the dough as evenly as possible into the baking sheet. Bake for 25–30 minutes. The dough will even out in the pan and hide imperfections. The top will appear bumpy while warm.

When the centre is set, remove the pan from the oven and wait 2–3 minutes before scoring it into shapes. Use any tool that will cut clean neat edges. After 5 minutes, repeat the scoring, making sure to press to the bottom of the pan. Cool until firm, then carefully transfer the cookies to a rack to cool until crisp.

Optional: Double Ginger Crispy Shortbread. Substitute 1 Tbsp. (15 mL) powdered sugar and 2 Tbsp. (30 mL) finely minced crystallized ginger for the cocoa and pepper.

Granny's Molasses Cookie Ice Cream Sandwiches

My grandmother Alvina's cookies are a legend in my family, so when I first tested them for this cookbook, it was a great shock to find out they weren't as good as I remember. When I mentioned this and how I had made some adjustments to the recipe at a family gathering, there were expressions of disbelief and dismay. This couldn't be! After much emotionally charged discussion we dug up Aunt Yvonne's version and I went back into the kitchen. This version is as good as I remember and I have stuffed them with ginger ice cream. My apologies to Granny and all of my relatives.

Makes 28 3-inch (7.5-cm) cookies or 14 ice cream sandwiches		Margaret Chisholm
1 cup	butter, softened to room temperature	240 mL
1 cup	sugar	240 mL
1	egg, slightly beaten	1
1 cup	molasses	240 mL
1/2 cup	strong coffee	120 mL
5 cups	all-purpose flour	1.2 L
1 tsp.	salt	5 mL
2 tsp.	ground cinnamon	10 mL
1/4 tsp.	ground cloves	1.2 mL
2 tsp.	ground ginger	10 mL.
1 Tbsp.	baking soda	15 mL
2 tsp.	baking powder	10 mL
12 Tbsp.	finely chopped candied ginger	180 mL
1 quart	high-quality vanilla ice cream	950 mL

Beat the butter in the bowl of an electric mixer until light. Add the sugar and beat until light and fluffy. Add the egg and beat until well combined. Add the molasses and coffee and beat until smooth. Mix together the flour, salt, spices, baking soda and baking powder. Add the flour mixture to the sugar mixture and mix by hand with a rubber spatula until smooth.

Scrape the dough into a ball, wrap with plastic wrap and chill for 1 hour to overnight.

Preheat the oven to 375°F (190°C). Roll the cookie dough out on a lightly floured board to 1/3 inch (.8 cm) thick. Cut with a 3-inch (7.5-cm) cookie cutter. Bake for 10 minutes or until puffed slightly, but still very soft in the centre. Transfer the cookies to a rack to cool.

When the cookies are completely cool, freeze them to prevent the ice cream melting as you make the sandwiches. Mix the ginger into slightly softened ice cream. Using a 1/4-cup (60-mL) ice cream scoop, place the ice cream on the bottom of a cookie, and place another cookie on top. Work quickly to fill all the cookies, and place the sandwiches in the freezer as you make them. Freeze for at least 1 hour before serving.

Secret

I love Häagen-Dazs ice cream. To be a fully realized experience, I need two flavours in the right kind of bowl with the right kind of spoon. Maple Walnut is a favourite, but hard to find, Chocolate Chocolate Chip and Caramel Cone Explosion make me introspective as I let each mouthful of ice cream melt away from its crunchy bits, and it is always nice to revisit Strawberry. As for the bowl and spoon, a small white rice bowl and a tiny espresso spoon make the experience complete.

—Karen Barnaby

Chocolate, Coconut and Lemon Macaroons

If I had to choose my favourite foods the top of my list would consist of chocolate, coconut and lemons. It is often difficult to find a recipe with all three together. These macaroons have a wonderful texture— crisp on the outside, soft and chewy on the inside.

Makes 20 cookies		Mary Mackay
3 oz.	semi-sweet chocolate, finely chopped	85 g
3	large egg whites, about 1/2 cup (120 mL)	3
1 Tbsp.	corn syrup	15 mL
2/3 cup	sugar	160 mL
3 Tbsp.	Dutch-process cocoa powder, sifted	45 mL
1 Tbsp.	lemon juice	15 mL
2 tsp.	finely chopped lemon zest	10 mL
1/4 tsp.	vanilla extract	1.2 mL
2 2/3 cups	unsweetened shredded coconut	635 mL
2 tsp.	all-purpose flour	10 mL

Preheat the oven to 350°F (175°C).

Heat a small pot of water until just simmering, then remove it from the heat. Place the finely chopped chocolate in a bowl and set it on top of the warm water, without letting the bowl touch the water. Stir the chocolate until it melts and set it aside to cool.

Place the egg whites, corn syrup, sugar, cocoa powder, lemon juice and lemon zest in a small pot. Whisk the mixture over medium-low heat until just warm. Stir in the melted chocolate and vanilla extract.

Toss the coconut and flour together in a bowl. Stir in the chocolate mixture.

Line a baking sheet with non-stick baking paper. Scoop heaping tablespoons of the mixture onto the non-stick baking paper, about 1 inch (2.5 cm) apart.

Bake until set on the outside but still soft on the inside, about 12–15 minutes. Slide the baking paper off the baking sheet and onto a rack to cool the cookies.

Secret

I have included my Award-Winning Biscotti Pears (page 142) not only because this truly is an award-winning dessert but also to set the story straight. I used to enjoy entering dessert competitions when I was pastry chef at Il Barino Restaurant in Vancouver. The Vancouver Playhouse International Wine Festival annually hosts a Quady Dessert Competition. Contestants had to submit a dessert to be paired with a Quady orange muscat wine called Essensia. I was aiming for the top prize, an all-inclusive trip to the Napa Valley in California. My dilemma was that you could only enter one dessert and I was torn between my Biscotti Pears and my Chocolate Zuccotto Cake.

With my eye on the prize, I could not choose between these two favourites, so I entered both, one in my name and one in my friend Richard's name. I was thrilled when the restaurant got a call to say that one of the desserts was in the top ten and they wanted us to bring samples to the Vintner's Brunch where they would be handing out awards in front of 500 people. Forget the trip to California—recognition for a young chef meant everything! My only problem was that it was the Biscotti Pears entered in Richard's name that they chose. So I prepared my 50 samples for the luncheon, and sadly watched Richard go up for his prize. I was not too upset that the Biscotti Pears did not take first place—just think how distressed I would have been if Richard had flown off to the Napa Valley!

—Mary Mackay

Pet Snacks

Biskitti

*This recipe makes tiny cat-sized biscotti—crunchie treats for your
loved ones. These biscotti are not like the ones we enjoy dunking in our
coffee. They are made with ground beef, chicken livers and fresh shrimp
meat. You can also just leave them raw instead of baking them. Your
furry friends will enjoy them just as much. This recipe has been tested
and approved by our tabbies Peppy and Pumpkin (a couple of the most
finicky eaters I know). Keep in mind these biskitti are only designed as
a treat and should not replace your
cat's regular diet.*

Makes about 50 biskitti		Mary Mackay
1 oz.	ground beef	28 g
1 oz.	fresh shrimpmeat	28 g
1 oz.	chicken liver	28 g
1 Tbsp.	grated Cheddar cheese	15 mL
1	egg yolk	1
1/2 tsp.	vegetable oil	2.5 mL
1 Tbsp.	water	15 mL
1/4 cup	brown rice flour	60 mL
1/3 cup	whole-wheat flour	80 mL
2 tsp.	each cornmeal and wheat germ	10 mL
1/8 tsp.	brewer's yeast	.5 mL
1/2 tsp.	dried catnip	2.5 mL

Preheat the oven to 350ºF (175ºC). Line a baking sheet with non-stick
baking paper.

Place the beef, shrimp, chicken liver, cheese, egg yolk, vegetable oil and
water in the bowl of a food processor. Using the steel knife, pulse for a few
seconds to purée. Add the rice flour, whole-wheat flour, cornmeal, wheat
germ and brewer's yeast and pulse until the dough comes together. It will be
moist and sticky.

Remove the dough from the bowl and knead for a couple of minutes on the
countertop. Divide the dough into 2 equal portions. Wet your hands with
a little water and roll each portion into a 12-inch (30-cm) log. Cut each
log into 25 pieces. Spread the biskitti out on the baking sheet. Bake for
20 minutes. Mist the tops of the biskitti with water and toss them in catnip.
Cool before serving.

Io's Food

Before deciding to make Io's food, I asked myself: What is that kibble stuff anyway and would I like to eat extruded pellets for the rest of my life? It is convenient for humans to serve, but not the best thing for a dog to eat. The effort has paid off well. She has a beautiful, shiny black coat, bright eyes and, unlike her mother, gets loads of compliments on her good looks and healthy glow. Besides this food, Io's diet is supplemented with the occasional piece of overcooked fish. I vary the grains by using millet, barley, 7-grain cereal, bulgur and quinoa. Sometimes I substitute lamb for the beef, or use half tofu or texturized vegetable protein (TVP) and half meat. After watching her eat grass, I tried sprouting wheat berries for part of the grain, but she enjoys eating grass more as a late night–walk snack.

Enough for 5 to 6 Doberman pinscher–sized meals		*Karen Barnaby*
1/2 lb.	raw whole grain	227 g
5 cups	water	1.2 L
8	Ester C (vitamin C) capsules	6
8	kyolic garlic pills	8
2 lbs.	extra-lean ground beef	900 g
1 lb.	grated raw carrots or zucchini	454 g
6 Tbsp.	flax seed oil or essential fatty acids oil blend	90 mL

Combine the grain and water in a large lidded pot. Bring to a boil, turn down to a simmer and cook for 1 hour, until the grain is very soft. Remove from the heat and cool until completely cold.

In a spice or coffee grinder, grind the Ester C and garlic pills to a powder. Combine with the grain, beef, carrots or zucchini and oil. Mix well. Keep refrigerated.

Mare's Munchies

Most pet lovers have tried their hand at making biscuits at some point for their beloved animals—but have you ever made horse cookies? My goddaughter's mother indulged my horse with these treats at Christmas. This is my version.

Makes 3 dozen		Lesley Stowe
1 cup	molasses	240 mL
1/2 cup	canola oil	120 mL
3 cups	whole wheat flour	720 mL
1/2 cup	oats (not oatmeal)	120 mL
1/2 cup	each grated carrot and apple	120 mL

Preheat the oven to 350°F (175°C). Mix the molasses and oil together. Add the flour, oats, carrot and apple. Drop by spoonfuls onto a greased cookie sheet. Flatten with a fork. Bake for 15 minutes.

Mom's Peanut Butter Sunflower Balls

This is my mother's recipe for feeding squirrels. Ever since my parents' cat Patate passed away they have taken to feeding some of the neighbourhood squirrels. They have gone so far as to name their new pets. There is Walnuts, who gets into my dad's shed and eats the stored walnuts. There is Blacky, because of his colouring. And there is One Eye for his . . . well, you know.

	Mary Mackay

Mom mixes together some natural unsalted peanut butter with shelled raw peanuts, shelled raw sunflower seeds and a little mixed birdseed. She forms it into a ball and puts it out on the squirrel feeder (yes, there really is such a thing as a squirrel feeder). Mom also recommends spreading the peanut butter mix on a dried cob of corn as an extra treat.

The Pantry

The Pantry List contains ingredients that a lot of our recipes have in common. With these grocery items on hand, and a quick shopping trip for fresh ingredients, you will be ready to cook at the drop of a hat, or frying pan.

In the Baking Cupboard

Amaretti cookies
Chestnuts, candied
Chocolate, semi-sweet
Chocolate, white
Cocoa powder, Dutch-process
Cornmeal
Cornstarch
Corn syrup
Cream of tartar
Flour, bread
Flour, pastry
Flour, unbleached white
Gelatin, granulated
Ginger, candied
Graham crumbs
Honey
Jam, apricot
Molasses
Oatmeal
Oats, rolled, large flake
Sugar, coarse or crystals
Sugar, dark brown
Sugar, granulated
Sugar, icing
Tapioca
Vanilla beans
Vanilla extract, pure
Wheat germ
Yeast, instant

Canned Goods

Artichoke hearts
Chickpeas
Corn, creamed
Corn, kernels
Fava beans
Tomato paste
Tomatoes, plum

Cheese and Dairy Products

Blue cheese
Camembert
Cheddar
Cream cheese
Feta
Goat's cheese, soft unripened
Gruyère, smoked
Mascarpone
Parmigiano Reggiano
Pecorino Romano
Provolone
Ricotta
St. André
Butter, unsalted
Crème fraîche
Sour cream
Yogurt

Condiments and Seasonings

Black beans, fermented
Chili sauce
Chinese cooking wine
Ketchup
Kikkoman memmi
Mirin
Mustard, Dijon and grainy
Oyster sauce
Piri piri sauce
Pomegranate molasses
Sambal oelek
Soy sauce
Steak sauce
Sweet chili sauce
Thai fish sauce
Truffle honey
Worcestershire sauce

Things Usually Found in the Fridge

Capers
Dill pickles
Horseradish, creamed
Mayonnaise, good quality
Olives, Kalamata and green
Pickled ginger
Pickled sweet cherry peppers
Sun-dried oil-packed tomatoes

Dried Goods

Black beans, dried
Couscous, Middle Eastern, toasted
Lentil du Puy
Mushrooms, dried porcini and morel
Rice, basmati and long-grained white
Rice papers
Soba noodles
Split green peas, dried

Fishy Stuff

Anchovy fillets
Caviar
Indian candy
Prawns, frozen
Salmon, smoked
Salt cod
Tuna, solid white and oil-packed

Fresh Stuff

Garlic
Ginger
Grapefruits
Lemons
Limes
Oranges
Onions, white and red
Shallots

Dried Fruit

Apricots
Blueberries, sun-dried
Cranberries, sun-dried
Currants
Dates
Figs, Black Mission and Calmyrna
Raisins, golden

In the Freezer

Corn
Fava beans
Phyllo pastry
Spring roll wrappers
Stock, chicken, meat and vegetable
Tortillas, flour
Wonton skins

Meaty Bits

Bacon, double-smoked
Pancetta
Prosciutto

Nuts and Seeds

Almonds, sugar-coated caramel
Almonds, whole, blanched, sliced
   and ground
Cashew pieces
Coconut, unsweetened: desiccated
   and large flake
Hazelnuts
Peanuts, roasted
Pecans
Pistachios, shelled
Pumpkin seeds
Sesame seeds, black and white
Walnuts

Oils

Canola
Olive, and extra virgin olive
Roasted grapeseed
Sesame
Truffle

Vinegars

Balsamic
Raspberry
Rice wine
Sherry vinegar
White wine

Herbs and Spices

Allspice, ground
Anise seeds
Bay leaves
Black mustard seeds
Cayenne pepper
Chili powder
Cinnamon sticks
Cinnamon, ground
Coriander seeds
Cumin, seeds and ground
Curry powder
Fennel seeds
Garlic powder
Garlic salt
Juniper berries
Mustard, dry
Oregano, Mexican
Paprika, hot, sweet and smoked
Peppers, dried: hot red flakes,
    chipotle peppers, pasilla peppers
    and ancho chili powder
Pepper, white
Peppercorns, whole black
Rosemary, dried
Saffron
Sea salt, fine and coarse
Thyme, dried
Turmeric
Wasabi, prepared and powdered

Alcohol

Armagnac
Beaumes de Venise (Muscat dessert
    wine)
Beer
Bourbon
Calvados
Cognac
Grand Marnier
Madeira
Marsala
Orange liqueur
Port
Rum
Scotch
Sherry, dry and sweet
Wine, dry red
Wine, dry white

And, just because it's good to have
    on hand . . . parchment paper.

Dishing It Up

Tapas-Style Dishing

If you like to leisurely nibble your way through a meal, you can create a large or small tapas-style dinner or appetizer spread from the following recipes. In general, keep complementary flavours, textures and colours in mind and plan for dishes that will be good to eat at room temperature. Most of these dishes can be prepared in advance with some last-minute fiddling. Serve with lots of good bread, small bowls of extra virgin olive oil and roasted almonds, and keep the wine or sherry flowing at a moderate pace.

Salt Cod "Seviche", page 21
Green Olives Baked with Sweet Sherry and Garlic, page 11
Roasted Red Onion and Shallot Tart with Thyme, page 10
Grilled Prawns with Smoked Pepper Tartar Sauce, page 128
Minted Feta Salad, page 55
Potato Salad with Tuna, Caper and Anchovy Vinaigrette, page 67
Summer Saffron Paella Salad, *The Girls Who Dish*, page 48
Tiger Mussels with Garlicky Focaccia Crumbs, page 30
Mediterranean Salad with Tapenade Vinaigrette, page 53
Pizzas Vertes, page 132
Roasted Beets with Tarragon Vinaigrette, page 56
Grilled Asparagus with Grapefruit Vinaigrette, page 59
Pepper Shooters, page 20

Dish a Picnic!

You don't really have to drive anywhere to have a picnic, just do it in your own backyard, balcony or living room. For that real picnic feeling, pack and drive the food around for an hour and import some ants. Picnic food should be portable, easy to eat, good at room temperature and require a minimum of dishes. Bring some fruit, bread and cheese, wet towels for wiping your hands on, and dig in!

Crunchy Baked "Tempura" Lemon Chicken, page 97
Bistro Slaw with Caramel Crunch Almonds, page 54
Cilantro Pesto Penne Salad, page 61
Roasted Two-Tomato Salad, *The Girls Who Dish*, page 42
Oatmeal Raisin Cake with Broiled Coconut Cashew Icing, page 170
Granny's Molasses Cookie Ice Cream Sandwiches, page 176

Elegant Italian Dishing

When you want to pull out all the stops, dish this elegant Italian dinner. Although porcini mushrooms are used twice, their flavour is very different. The porcini dust on the sea bass is mysterious and smoky and on the crostini, rich and smooth. Serve with My Mother's Pre-Biscotti Biscotti, page 174, and slivers of Parmesan cheese with the dessert wine. By the way, porcini means little pig in Italian.

Porcini Mushroom Mascarpone Crostini, page 3
Butternut Squash and Fava Bean Soup with Truffle Oil, page 38
Porcini-Dusted Sea Bass with Balsamic Brown Butter, page 124
Gnocchi with Walnut Pesto, page 16
Honey and Thyme Roasted Winter Vegetables, page 79
Braised Red Onions Wrapped in Pancetta,
The Girls Who Dish, page 132
Candied Chestnut Semifreddo with Chocolate Sauce, page 152

Far East Dishing

The focus is on spice in this far east collection of dishes. Serve cups of sweet, creamy chai with dessert.

Curry-Crusted Leg of Lamb with Cumin Raita, page 109
Tomatoes Baked Beneath Spiced Onions, page 74
Roasted Carrots with Saffron Chili Oil, page 75
Cucumber Salad with Peanuts, Coconut and Lime, page 52
Toasted Coconut Rice with Spice and Raisins, page 88
Gingered Apricots with Mascarpone in Pistachio Tuilles, page 140

Virtuous Vegetable Dishing

The difficulty that is most often found with planning vegetarian meals is that there is no meat as the focal point. Instead of vegetables in the supporting role, they become the stars. Instead of having one star, all the elements can become stars. Balance a vegetable-based meal with complementary flavours and textures.

Mediterranean Salad with Tapenade Vinaigrette, page 53
Green Chickpea Ratatouille, page 80
Roasted Carrots with Saffron Chili Oil, page 75
Après-Ski Skillet of Potatoes, Peppers and Feta, page 83
Roasted Beets with Tarragon Vinaigrette, page 56
Parfait Mon Cherry, *The Girls Who Dish*, page 150

Comfort Dishing

If you want to make the world go away . . . cook.

Deep Dish Chicken Phyllo Tart, page 98
Chipotle Bourbon Cranberry Sauce, page 103
Fennel Mashed Potatoes, *The Girls Who Dish*, page 126
Cardamom Apple Cake, page 169

Elegant Seafood Dishing

While these menus consist of only four items each, the overall effect will create oohs, ahhs and many kudos.

Crab Cakes with Watercress and Roast Curry Vinaigrette, page 24
Salmon with Sautéed Vegetables and Balsamic Butter Sauce, page 120
White Bean and Garlic Mousse, *The Girls Who Dish*, page 137
Gingered Apricots with Mascarpone in Pistachio Tuilles, page 140

Spicy Jumbo Prawns with Nutty Herb Sauce, page 26
Fire-Crusted Sea Bass with Citrus Mango Relish, page 122
Skillet-Braised Caramelized Fennel, *The Girls Who Dish*, page 143
Stu's Mascarpone "Cheesecake" with Plum Compote, page 156

Spicy Seafood Dishing

Grilled Prawns with Smoked Pepper Tartar Sauce, page 128
Chili-Crusted Cod on a Bed of Braised Lentils, page 116
Asian Greens Tuscan Style, *The Girls Who Dish*, page 145
Sabayon of Beaumes de Venise with Armagnac Winter Fruit, page 144

Simple Seafood Dishing

Halibut and "Chips," page 115
Bistro Slaw with Caramel Crunch Almonds, page 54
Golden Oven Fries, page 86
Granny's Molasses Cookie Ice Cream Sandwiches, page 176

Simple Dinner Dishing

In our everyday lives, we don't usually prepare a multi-course dinner as a daily event. Here are a few fast suggestions when you want something that is a bit more than the norm. When you plan dinners, consider breaking out of the comfort zone of meat, starch and vegetables on the plate and incorporating a salad instead of the vegetables or just two complementary items together on the plate. Here are a few of our favourites.

Jerk Chicken with Cucumber Lime Salsa, page 95
Cumin-Roasted Yams, *The Girls Who Dish*, page 127

Turkey Breast with Chipotle Bourbon Cranberry Sauce, page 102
Asian Greens Tuscan Style, *The Girls Who Dish*, page 145

Springtime Open-Face Asparagus Sandwich, page 6
Warm Red Cabbage Salad with Pancetta and Hazelnuts, page 69

Thai Salad Niçoise, page 58
Grilled Asparagus with Sesame Drizzle, page 72

Tiger Mussels with Garlicky Focaccia Crumbs, page 30
Minted Feta Salad, page 55

Grilled Portobello and Steak in Asian Marinade, page 108
Cucumber Salad with Peanuts, Coconut and Lime, page 52

Pacific Rim-Style Dishing

Grilled Portobello and Steak in Asian Marinade, page 108
Asian Green Beans, page 81
Grilled Asparagus with Sesame Drizzle, page 72
Steamed Rice
Lemon Meringue Kisses, page 167

Blow-Out Buffet Dishing

Return all those dinner invitations you've been putting off.

Crispy Saint André and Leek Wedges, page 8
Breast of Chicken with Morels and Cranberries, page 92
Grilled Asparagus with Grapefruit Vinaigrette, page 59
Balsamic Spuds, *The Girls Who Dish*, page 125
Fifteen Minutes of Fame Chocolate Torte, page 166
Crispy Chocolate and Black Pepper Shortbread, page 175

Sunday Dinner Dishing

When you want to spend a slow and lazy day cooking. Make a double batch of soup to have some for a weekday dinner.

Roasted Garlic and Pumpkin Soup with Five-Spice Crèma, page 39
Pomegranate Roast Lamb, page 114
Minted Feta Salad, page 55
Golden Oven Fries, page 86
Award-Winning Biscotti Pears with Caramel Sauce, page 142

Roast Squash and Pear Soup, page 36
Sauté of Chicken with Gorgonzola and Fresh Herbs, page 94
Horseradish Mashed Potatoes with Spinach, page 85
Rhubarb and Strawberry Crumble, page 162

A Big Bunch of Barbecue Dishing

We are always looking for a way to beat the heat in the summer, and a way to bring barbecuing to new heights of fashion. The list on the following page contains the most suitable recipes for barbecue thrills. Remember to check out Margaret's Trio of Dry Rubs, page 136.

Appetizers

Grilled Mushroom, Eggplant and Olive Flatbread, page 4
Chèvre and Pear Quesadillas with Cilantro Crema, page 14
Double Tomato Bruschetta, *The Girls Who Dish*, page 6
Tomato Prawn Bruschetta, *The Girls Who Dish*, page 21

Fish and Seafood

Grilled Prawns with Smoked Pepper Tartar Sauce, page 128
Grilled Prawns and Prosciutto with Basil Sauce, *The Girls Who Dish*, page 73
Coriander Prawns with Sun-dried Tomato Coulis and
Pineapple Mango Relish, *The Girls Who Dish*, page 74
Sweet BBQ Salmon, Rivers Inlet Style, *The Girls Who Dish*, page 78
Ahi Tuna Niçoise, *The Girls Who Dish*, page 47

Meat

Jerk Chicken with Cucumber Lime Salsa, page 95
Grilled Portobello and Steak in Asian Marinade, page 108
Red-Cooked Lamb Shanks with Star Anise and Ginger, page 110
Curry-Crusted Leg of Lamb with Cumin Raita, page 109
Lamb Salad with Crushed Peanuts and Lime Dressing,
The Girls Who Dish, page 51
Mustard and Herb-Crusted Lamb Chops,
The Girls Who Dish, page 111

Vegetables

Grilled Endive, page 73
Grilled Asparagus with Grapefruit Vinaigrette, page 59
Fresh Herb Salad with Grilled Mushrooms and Tomatoes,
The Girls Who Dish, page 38
Grilled Fresh Artichokes with Roasted Garlic Aïoli,
The Girls Who Dish, page 138
Portobello Mushroom Skewers on Wild Greens,
The Girls Who Dish, page 131
Grilled Caesar Salad with Parmesan Crisps and Reggiano Shavings,
The Girls Who Dish, page 40
Grilled Portobello Mushrooms with Watercress and Pecan Pesto,
The Girls Who Dish, page 130

Index of Recipes by Chef

Index

About the Photographer

Greg Athans is one of Vancouver's premier food and beverage photographers. He has operated a large downtown studio since the mid-1980s and has shot many cookbooks, including multiple award winners in Canada and the USA. His clients include Nabisco, White Spot, Calona Wines, Milestone's, Hy's, Red Robin, Fletcher's Fine Foods, Original Cakerie, Corby, Okanagan Spring Brewery, Bread Garden, Joe Fortes, and The Fish House. Greg Athans can be reached at (604) 873-6650.